LETTERS
TO MY
WHITE
MALE
FRIENDS

Also by Dax-Devlon Ross

Make Me Believe

The Nightmare and the Dream

The Underdog's Manifesto

A Staircase of Words

The Best of Intentions

Beat of a Different Drum

LETTERS

TO MY

WHITE

MALE

FRIENDS

DAX-DEVLON ROSS

ST. MARTIN'S PRESS

New York

Author's Note:

This is a true story, though some names have been changed.

First published in the United States by St. Martin's Press,
an imprint of St. Martin's Publishing Group

www.stmartins.com

Design by Donna Sinisgalli Noetzel

Library of Congress Cataloging-in-Publication Data

Names: Ross, Dax-Devlon, author.
Title: Letters to my white male friends / Dax-Devlon Ross.
Description: First edition. | New York : St. Martin's Press, 2021. |
    Includes bibliographical references.
Identifiers: LCCN 2020057563 | ISBN 9781250276834 (hardcover) |
    ISBN 9781250276841 (ebook)
Subjects: LCSH: United States—Race relations. | Race awareness. |
    African American men—Washington (D.C.)—Biography. |
    Racism—United States. | Men, White—United States—Attitudes.
Classification: LCC HT1561 .R67 2021 | DDC 305.800973—dc23
LC record available at https://lccn.loc.gov/2020057563

Our books may be purchased in bulk for promotional,
educational, or business use. Please contact your local
bookseller or the Macmillan Corporate and Premium Sales
Department at 1–800-221-7945, extension 5442, or by email at
MacmillanSpecialMarkets@macmillan.com.

First Edition: 2021

10 9 8 7 6 5 4 3 2 1

To my two forever loves, Lana and Ella.

Lana, thank you for introducing me

to myself again.

We can learn to work and speak when we are afraid in the same way we have learned to work and speak when we are tired. For we have been socialized to respect fear more than our own needs for language and definition . . .

—AUDRE LORDE

I

HARM

INTRODUCTION

I will never forget one night in Cape Town when I was out at a dance club with a group of fellow law students. My friends and I were clustered by the bar, spending our overvalued cash with an all-too-eager-to-please barkeep, talking loudly as Americans often do without even wondering if it's obnoxious, when I noticed something unusual out of the corner of my eye. Picture this scene with me. The dance floor was dark and crowded, thick with grinding bodies. But there was one body—the one that caught my attention—moonwalking around the perimeter of the floor in its own orbit. How often do you see anyone in a club moonwalking? It isn't the type of dance that one performs alone in a club. I'm not certain that it can even be classified, in the classic sense of the word, as dance; it's more like a move within a dance. Something that precedes a spin and drop-down split.

I couldn't get over what I was witnessing. I nudged my friends, who looked over and chuckled before returning to their conversation. Not me, though. I decided to climb to the balcony overlooking the dance floor so I could look down on this mysterious moonwalker. Round and round he went without stopping. After his third or fourth circum-navigation, my laughter petered out and something else started to emerge. The moonwalker didn't give a damn. Whoever was watching or whatever people thought had nothing whatsoever to do with him.

Why begin these letters to you with an anecdote about a stranger I witnessed moonwalking in a club twenty years ago? What possible connection does that experience have to race?

The simplest way I can put it is that at that point in my life I believed, whether or not I was ready to admit it to myself, that there was a single standard of the successful and therefore acceptable Black man, and either I met that standard or my life was a failure. A successful and acceptable Black man had a clean record, credentials from the most prestigious institutions that would have him, and a career in a field that white America held in high regard. He rose above his race, excelling without complaint or excuse. He spoke with perfect anglophone diction and dressed impeccably though conservatively. Most important, he was always on time.

But I knew another side of that Black man.

He was, also, trapped in a role he was assigned to play in order to survive and gain some measure of stature and stability in a hypercompetitive, hyper-individualistic society. He was my dad. He was so many of the Black men I grew up around. Collectively, they were my first heroes. I just couldn't live their Black lives. For them, succeeding in newly integrated America depended on their ability to swallow racial slights with a straight face and keep climbing the ladder. It hinged on how well they tempered their Black cultural identity and mimicked the white middle-class cultural norms that most workplaces rest upon. Whatever unconventional or nontraditional life paths they might have longed to pursue had to be surrendered for the more noble cause of advancing the race on white America's timeline.

Witnessing this as a kid, I became resentful of the stirring sense that if I wanted any kind of respectable future, I had no choice but to fit into a Black-male mold meant to manage the anxieties of white people. Doing so would have been inauthentic to my experience inside white spaces, where, for better and worse, I had been reared since middle school. No one told my white male friends that they needed to be a credit to the race. They weren't taught to code switch so they could assimilate and appear competent. Rather, they were groomed to govern, treated as individuals, and assured ever so subtly that they were the standard by which everyone else was measured. And because I was there as well, right beside them, I received the same education. Consequently, comporting myself to white America's standards of success to advance the race did not appeal to me. It would have required me to repudiate a part of my experience, blot it out, which struck me as a most vicious act of self-betrayal, a twisted kind of self-hatred.

Selfishly, I couldn't go on harboring the resentment and rage inside. I was angry with my parents' generation for settling for middle-class crumbs. Angry at my Black peers for not being angry enough. And angry with white people for comfortably and obliviously wielding dominion over it all as if it were an ordained right.

Even then I knew quite well that all of that anger would eventually poison my well. I'd seen bitterness ruin Black lives. Seen it sprawled on street corners, slumped over bar counters, and strewn across the entire American landscape. I knew I needed to create my own Black life that included white people not just as coworkers I joked with superficially and neighbors I waved to but distrusted and kept my distance from. I needed to be able to hold white people close as fellow, flawed travelers on an imperfect journey toward justice and healing. One that I might not live long enough to see the end of. But for that to happen, I still had searching that I needed to do, questions I needed to answer, feelings I needed to reconcile. Maybe you can relate. Maybe, friend, at a similar age you also felt as if you had to make a choice between invention and convention, between hunkering down and remaining open despite the storms ahead. For me, the mysterious moonwalker became a liberation metaphor. At critical life junctures over the next twenty years, his image reemerged to guide me on my path into the unknown. *Go. Live. Take the risk. Be bold. Make your own way. It will be okay. You will be okay.*

The book you are holding is not a handbook on how to be anti-racist. That book exists. This is also not an attempt to exploit anyone's pity or guilt. Nor do I want to call out, humiliate, or shame anyone. To be sure, I employ my personal and professional journey to illuminate and illustrate larger societal events and trends that have shaped a generation's story. My journey has placed me in proximity to the criminal justice system, recent social-justice movements, the non-profit industry, urban development, urban education, and workplace diversity and inclusion. I have thus spent my career thinking, reporting, writing, and otherwise working to reform the inequitable systems, practices, and policies that many of you, maybe for the first time, are encountering and grappling with as parts of a broader system that protects and exalts white advantage. In my experience, this *inexperience* has led my white friends and colleagues to often name problems and propose solutions for Black people without understanding context or appreciating the extent to which those views and solutions stem from an unexamined acceptance of certain truths about the society we inhabit.

I write the letters herein to my white male friends because you are everyone's target but no one's focus. You and I both know that you hold immense power, wealth, and status in our society. That power strikes fear and invokes intimidation. It instills a sense of incontestable authority and certainty. Consequently, no one ever speaks to you directly. No one challenges you to push beyond your comfort zones. In short, when it comes to conversations about race, white men are typically coddled and appeased.

For us to collectively move toward racial healing and justice, you are going to have to reckon with your role not just in what has been wrought but in what we are building. Are you prepared to deconstruct the citadels that have granted you power, privilege, and authority? Are you going to go along with scrapping the constructs that have sustained your cultural dominance? Are you willing to break up the cabals that keep the best colleges and careers for your children? Are you going to accept and embrace a new multiracial coalition led by the Black women who fueled Joe Biden's victory in 2020? Will you adapt yourselves and your organizations to meet the demands (because they won't just be requests anymore) for inclusion and equity? Will you be able to remake the institutions and arrangements that have made you wealthy and privileged into ones that bring prosperity to all? Will you be willing to evolve your tried-and-true beliefs about how the world works, how cities are designed, how communities thrive, how people succeed? Will you accept higher taxes and lower returns on your investments, more competition from people who couldn't previously get into the room?

These are the questions that we have always found ourselves getting stuck on. In previous moments of upheaval, the white men in charge at the time were unwilling to engage in good faith with Black people on the hard questions about how we are going to organize our society and sincerely spread opportunity. They instead chose, time and again, accommodation and reform around the edges. They decided what they were willing to share with Black people and then decided that their offer was fair. They offered just enough access and opportunity for Black people to satiate the moment, but not enough to disrupt the status quo. And then, after a few years, they decided that they had done enough to ameliorate generations of suffering and exploitation. They pushed and rolled back gains. They defunded programs. They reasserted their dominance. That has been our model for racial reckoning to date. That model can't be reformed. It needs to be blown up.

If we are going to survive together, you will not be able to decide for everyone else how society shall function. And I believe the only way that you will be able to embrace our new shared reality is if you can come to believe it's best for everyone, including you.

Whether you will be okay with the upheaval afoot is still very much an open question. I have no doubt some, many, of you will resist. But I for one have come to believe this is the only way. And I also believe that at least some white men of my generation are ready to take bold action to complete the work we were falsely informed had been finalized with school integration followed by civil rights legislation advancing opportunity for my people. In the past year I have been in conversation with dozens of white men from different walks who are awakening to the realization that, maybe, simply not being racist isn't enough to end racism. These men want deeper insight not only into how racism has harmed Black people, but, for the first time, into how it has harmed them. They are beginning to see that racism warps us all. The maladies merely manifest differently on the dominant group than on the subordinates.

A word about structure. This book stems from an essay I wrote at the dawn of the George Floyd protests. Without intending it, that essay struck a chord with white men caught between baby boomers and millennials and who are often forgotten about as a consequence. Men I had never met were moved to reach out to me, and I was grateful to listen. As I did (and read their messages), a pattern emerged. They acknowledged that they, too, had experienced **harm**. Then expressed a desire to **heal**. Then they asked for advice on how to **act**.

This book's three parts reflect those three themes. In the letters in Part I, I revisit my socialization inside white-dominant institutions starting in seventh grade. My intention is to attune you to your own racialization—because whether you were aware of it or not, it happened. At various points of our youth, you and I both received messages about who belonged and who didn't, who was worthy and who wasn't. Unexamined, these messages formed beliefs that guided my life and yours. My hope is that these letters will help you revisit your youth with a different lens.

Part II traces my long, rocky racial-healing journey through early adulthood into early middle age to guide seekers who wish to do their own healing work. In each letter I grapple with one overarching attribute of white-dominant culture that I encountered and have come to believe stands in the way of white people finding true fellowship and common cause with Black people.

Part III offers some historical and contemporary perspective as well as practical guidance and tools for taking action at work, in your community, and within yourself in ways that don't reinforce and reproduce the very harms we are seeking to ameliorate. I intentionally resist offering prescriptions and pat solutions, because there are none. The work you choose to do is context specific and dynamic. It is ongoing and evolving. Finally, my aim is to call in those who are ready to put in work for the long haul. If you identify with that call to action, then this book is for you.

Friend,

I have a distinct memory of the phone call. My sister Candace announced that Dad wanted a word. By then Dad had been out of the house for three years. Another story, another time. When I entered her room, Candace was dangling the phone in my direction and grinning fiendishly.

"He has some news," she ominously declared.

I snatched the phone and waited for her to leave. Then I made sure the door was closed and took a deep breath.

A few months earlier Dad had picked me up early one Saturday morning and driven me to Archbishop Carroll High School, where I'd sat alongside dozens of other kids my age in the school's basement cafeteria taking what felt like a daylong exam, the results of which would, in part, determine whether I got admitted to a private school. Although we'd discussed a few options, to Dad the only one that mattered was Sidwell Friends.

For Dad, Sidwell offered opportunities that he could never have dreamed of for himself as a boy growing up in segregated Richmond, Virginia, in the 1940s and '50s. He was also a futurist who loved *Star Trek* and repeatedly rented Stanley Kubrick's *2001: A Space Odyssey* from our local video store, a cavernous neighborhood joint called Errol's. Looking back, I can say with confidence that he viewed Sidwell as my ticket into a still-evolving, integrated America that he knew he would never be able to fully access himself. Growing up under Jim Crow and attending historically Black Howard University meant he hadn't been able to build deep cross-racial relationships as a young person. As for his career, as far as I knew, all of his colleagues were other Black engineers. I can't recall him having even a single white friend or associate.

For me, Sidwell was a sort of reluctant rite of passage. The coolest boys in Washington, D.C.'s Shepherd Park neighborhood went there. Chris Owens. Sam Simpson. Nick Robinson. Watt Gregory. Marcus Berry. They were all only a few years ahead of me, but in my mind they were towering figures who moved effortlessly about our neighborhood in their parents' fly whips and shimmering Sidwell-emblazoned gear. They were spoken about by others—parents, boys, girls, whoever—like rap stars. Even in our middle-class neighborhood, which I later learned was itself an anomaly, these boys were clearly the anointed. And because they all owned the same air of casual indifference that I had only witnessed in Brat Pack films up to that point, I deduced that the Sidwell mystique was at play.

My fascination—indeed obsession—with Sidwell was

further stoked by my having happened to attend the public elementary school directly across the street. I say "happened" because Phoebe Hearst Elementary wasn't anywhere near my neighborhood. It sat in D.C.'s whitest zip code.[1] I was there as a matter of both convenience and future consideration. My oldest sister, Leslie Amina, was a student at Duke Ellington School of the Arts, which was just a few klicks down Wisconsin Avenue from Hearst. Having us in proximity meant she could drive me to school and, in a pinch, pick me up if necessary. Separately, Hearst fed into Alice Deal Junior High Middle School, which then fed into Woodrow Wilson High School. At the time both were widely considered among D.C.'s best public schools. Yet, despite the neighborhood's demography and proximity to "good" public schools, white children were relatively absent from my classrooms. I'd venture to say at least half my Hearst classmates were, like me, "out-of-zone" Black children.

How could that be?

A couple of explanations come to mind and, perhaps, provide some context. First, Generation X was (and, thus, naturally remains) a relatively small generational cohort in comparison to boomers and millennials.[2] The late sixties and seventies were marred by the Vietnam War, social unrest, and stagflation, all of which contributed to plummeting birth rates.[3] At the same time, white people, especially, were leaving D.C. in droves. Between 1950 and 1990 the D.C. population declined by 25 percent—more than two hundred thousand people.[4] *Can we just sit with that for a moment?* At the exact moment *Brown v. Board of Education* and accompanying civil rights legislation kicked in and Black people started making gains in D.C., white people jumped ship. They either sent their kids to a private school or moved to a suburb. That's how much of a threat we posed. How little interest white parents had in their children being educated alongside kids who looked like me.

D.C. wasn't an outlier in this regard. In Maryland and Michigan, white voters overwhelmingly chose Alabama governor George Wallace in the 1972 Democratic presidential primaries *solely* because of his explicitly racist antibusing rhetoric.[5] In 1974, the same white parents who surely opposed the vicious treatment of Black schoolchildren in the Deep South infamously rioted in Boston when the courts enforced a busing system to desegregate schools.[6]

So, when you ask me what you can do, I am going to ask you throughout these letters to reckon with our not-so-distant past. Even after the successful struggles for civil rights and the proclamation that we had overcome, even as we were learning about Rosa Parks and *Brown v. Board* in school, your parents did not want you to go to school with me. They did everything in their power to resist my presence. And when they couldn't fight it anymore, they left. I'm sure that if you were to ask them why they did this, they would tell you it was about local control and their liberty interests, the overarching American ideal of individual rights. They will tout the fruits of meritocracy—that they should have the right to use their hard-earned wealth as they see fit without government interference. They will insist that you, as a parent, would have done the same. They will deny that race was a factor. In those moments, it is on you to challenge the color-blind narratives your parents peddle. Share data with them. Use facts. You may not change their minds, but at least you will be clearer about your past and more equipped to be honest with yourself when the pull to separate your children from mine feels strongest.

To be sure, white parents didn't undo the promise of school desegregation alone. They were wind-aided by a backlash against the rights revolution that Martin Luther King warned "succeeds every period of progress" in his 1967 book, *Where Do We Go from Here: Chaos or Community?* When Richard Nixon gained control of the White House just one year later, he quickly set about dismantling the liberal Supreme Court, which had brought about sweeping victories for the poor, workers, and people of color. In five and a half years, he appointed four conservative justices (by comparison, Barack Obama had just two appointments in his *eight* years) who in tandem reshaped the America we would grow up in. In 1973, the new Supreme Court reversed a lower-court decision that would have made equal funding for all students the law of the land.[7] In 1974, it reversed a lower-court decision that extended school busing desegregation efforts into suburbs.[8] Both were 5–4 decisions with strong dissents from Thurgood Marshall, who had argued the *Brown* case two decades earlier for the NAACP. Perversely, even after Nixon's crooked behind was run out of Washington, his appointees continued to run the Court and, consequently, shape the course of our education. A half century later, Donald Trump's three conservative Supreme Court appointments (Gorsuch, Kavanaugh, and Barrett) during his single, tumultuous term point to a similarly dim civil rights horizon for our children.

None of what had already taken place in the courts registered in my world or yours, not in real time. By the time we were ready for middle school, these momentous rulings were already firmly embedded, and Martin Luther King's birthday was a national holiday. We were just kids navigating a post–civil rights childhood on our separate planes of existence.

Waiting for the tests results while sitting in Sidwell's shadow was torture. Every day, whether during recess or while playing kickball after school, I'd glance over at the shimmering fortress and wonder what it was like inside those walls. Sidwell stood, quite literally, on a hill behind a tall cement wall. From wherever I stood, I could only see the fence straddling the track, which ringed the football field. I could hear whistles blowing and fans cheering. Could see the legs and feet of runners rounding their final bend or long jumpers careening through the sky. On a really lucky day, I'd notice one of the neighborhood boys walking to his car. I'd call after him and he'd shoot me a knowing nod or wave. On one occasion soon after I took the test, I ran up to one of those boys and announced my intention of joining him the following year. He just looked at me and said, "Good luck."

All of that hope and anxiety sat in my chest as I placed the chunky cordless to my ear that evening.

"Hey," I said, steeling myself for the worst. I pictured the embarrassment and shame of being rejected. Having to walk the neighborhood knowing I wasn't good enough to get in.

"You did it," Dad said without dragging out my anticipation. "You got in."

As clear as my memory is of the events leading up to that specific moment, everything thereafter isn't even a blur. I genuinely don't recall it. I don't know if I was calm or if I yelled. Did I run through the house? Did I go tell my mother? I just don't know.

What I know is that gaining acceptance into Sidwell Friends remains one of the most important moments of my life. It was incredibly validating. I was a hard worker and a quick learner. I never missed a homework assignment and often sought additional work. In the summers, I studied Candace's math textbooks on my own so I would be ready for the upcoming school year. In fifth grade, I was one of eight children—four white, four Black—placed into sixth-grade classes. Even then, I excelled. Similarly, I liked to perform, whether on the court, in the classroom, or in our school's annual plays. One year I played the Cowardly Lion in our production of *The Wiz*. Another year I played Bob Cratchit in *A Christmas Carol*. I was a lieutenant crossing guard, class vice president. I volunteered at a local senior citizens home. I had friends upon friends. Nothing gave me more joy than playing soccer and reading comic books.

Friend, I tell you all of this because I need you to have a sense of who I was before I entered your world. I need you to know that even though my parents split, my dad stuck close, and I remained, by and large, a happy, engaged, outgoing kid. I was not sullen. I was not withdrawn and disengaged. I did not struggle academically and didn't stir trouble in school. I still remember calling a fellow classmate "fag" in third grade. My teacher, Mrs. Powers, made me issue an apology to the entire class the following day. To this day, I don't know where those words came from or why I felt compelled to humiliate another human being. That memory has never left me and never will. It is one of the reasons I work to create empathy and understanding between people and groups now.

Back then I wasn't narrowly focused on basketball as my golden ticket, my one respite. I didn't freestyle because I wanted to be a rapper; I enjoyed boasting with words for fun. *For fun*. Too often, the narrative about boys who look like me—the one we as a society tell and tell and tell— suggests that your people and your institutions saved, uplifted, and enlightened me. That without you, my woebegone Black ass would be lost. I just need you to know that I existed fully and completely long before I entered your world.

I also need you to know where I come from. For your parents, the civil rights era might have ended with Dr. King's assassination, but for mine the movement still pulsated on WHUR, in the Black art inside our homes, and in places such as D.C.'s Carter Barron Amphitheatre each summer. We had a Malcolm X print in the hallway that for years I thought was my dad. Bobby Seale, the cofounder of the Black Panther Party, lived around the corner for a time. But I was not ducking bullets and dodging drug dealers in Shepherd Park. I never had to worry about food or where I would live. We took family vacations to Martha's Vineyard and Jamaica. We were in Jack and Jill, though I hated it and dropped out the moment my mother stopped forcing me to attend events. I knew dozens of real-life Huxtables before the Huxtables were even a thing. The streets in Shepherd Park were quiet and safe, tree-lined and wide enough to play football in the evening. We organized our own massive games of manhunt (think tag on steroids) that lasted all day long and spanned the entire neighborhood. We raced bikes through the alleys that snaked through the neighborhood like tributaries. We trekked through Rock Creek Park. We rode sleds down the big hill at Shepherd playground. More than a few kids had in-ground pools with diving boards. The Freemans had a tennis court, basketball court, *and* a pool in their backyard.

The white people that I knew lived in *our* neighborhood.

The Doyles—three Irish boys around my age, Brennan, Connor, and Dillon—were among my closest friends in part because the fiberglass hoop in the alley behind their house was the site of our neighborhood pickup games. After school I played Beastie Boys tapes until soccer practice at the house of blond-haired, blue-eyed Finn Doggert. Timothy Yip, Josh Bigelow, and Paul Riorko were the other white boys on our team. The rest of us were Black or what we then called mixed, the more palatable *biracial* having not yet been invented. Our coach, Mr. Holmes, was a Black executive at Honeywell. Finn's stepdad—also blond, albeit thinning—was the de facto assistant even though none of us listened to him. Coach Holmes—an old-school yeller and chronic ear plucker—ran our team with an iron fist. Also, Finn talked mad shit to his stepdad. We'd never seen a kid punk his pops to his face, let alone in public. To us, that was some quintessential white-people nonsense. Our Black fathers weren't playing that. They'd found a way out of their childhood circumstances and back home from Vietnam. Now their little Black sons were playing soccer with little white boys on a big-ass field in a leafy, predominantly Black neighborhood in a predominantly Black city. It didn't occur to me until much later in life to wonder what it must've been like for them, after growing up under

Jim Crow, to watch us run around together. Or what it cost them to hold at bay the world they knew awaited us.

The biggest threat to my young life wasn't the police or a stray bullet. It was an older kid we called, simply, Black Moe because his skin was so dark. He menaced me in particular because, as he later put it, I needed to get some heart. Moe would snatch my Mongoose and ride it around the neighborhood until he was finished having his fun for the day. Then he'd leave the bike somewhere for me to find. Moe would punch me so hard in the arm that I couldn't lift it for an hour. Moe would punk me out of my 7-Eleven Slurpee money and then drink one in front of me. But Moe also had my back when a group of boys from nearby Takoma Park chased us home after we smashed them in a basketball tournament on their home turf. He made sure I got home safe and sound, then he rounded up some of the older heads in the neighborhood for a good old-fashioned brawl at the local 7-Eleven.

I never felt my Black experience mattered to America. I rarely saw it presented on-screen or celebrated in print, therefore I assumed no one cared to hear what someone such as me had to say. In America, whenever the subject of race is broached, we immediately think of people struggling from deficits, gaps, and lack rooted in economic inequality and racial injustice. Over time, I came to understand that my story doesn't support the narrative that white saviorism is built on. When I worked as a nonprofit fundraiser especially, I learned to use my special access and presumed proximity to the struggle to benefit those really in need. But in doing so I also suppressed the validity of my own struggle. I realize that I have done a disservice to us both. You need to understand that the story you have been told and continue to tell about us is missing a major chapter. The post–civil rights era brought significant gains for Black people. Before we walked it all back, we walked this very road we are on now toward racial justice. And despite the dogma that Reaganites assert to the contrary, the federal government's role (War on Poverty, affirmative action) was the linchpin to those gains. The African American poverty rate nearly halved (58 percent to 30 percent) between 1959 and 1975, the year I was born.[9] Similarly, the US Department of Labor found that between 1974 and 1980, businesses contracting with the government raised minority employment by 20 percent. (During that same period, minority employment only rose by 12 percent in companies that did not contract with the government.)[10]

My parents were those "minorities" who benefited from policies aimed at redressing past harm and leveling the playing field. Opportunities afforded by civil rights legislation allowed my dad to win government contracts that in turn allowed him to start a business, buy homes, build wealth, and send me to a school such as Sidwell. After the divorce, those same protections gave my mother a pathway to employment that allowed us to stay in our home and not backslide into poverty.

Against this backdrop, it should be no surprise that D.C. became Chocolate City. It was among a handful of cities in America where Black folks could truly thrive; where a regular kid such as me could come of age believing that Black people were the center of the universe, such that when my sixth-grade teacher, Mrs. Loman, announced one day that African Americans only comprised 14 percent of the US population, I sat in quiet disbelief. *That just isn't possible.* The mayor and most of the city council were Black. Dad was a Howard alum, so I grew up on the Yard thinking that all colleges were HBCUs. Across town, "Big" John Thompson was the coach at Georgetown, which, at the time, had the blackest, baddest basketball team in America. I hope you can see that, for me and for a whole lot of other people who share the racial categorization Black in "the District," as we called it—extra emphasis on the *D*—back then, Black didn't mean "lack." We weren't suffering. We were intact. And our Black parents deserve all of the credit for that. They did that, *together*. Certainly, plenty of Black folks had preceded them—thriving Black diasporic communities is not a new story. Ivan Van Sertima's *They Came Before Columbus* forcefully argues that Africans arrived in the New World long before Columbus. Van Sertima grounds his entire thesis in archaeological evidence, in the very science that I know you find necessary to validate an argument's legitimacy. So even if you aren't convinced, you can't dismiss it out of hand as counterfactual.

The dozens and dozens and *dozens* of thriving Black families I grew up surrounded by were, and very much understood themselves to be, a community. They came from different places—the Deep South, the Midwest, the Caribbean—but they found each other, exchanged the nod, and together constructed a loose confederation that for a delicate few and now-forgotten years became a cocoon of safety and support for their kids. They understood in ways we, their children, couldn't, how dangerous and delicate the thing they were building was. They had seen Emmett Till's mangled little body in *Jet* magazine. My dad was born just one month after Till in 1941, smack-dab in the middle of World War II. I know now that so much of his fear for my life traced back to seeing that poor boy's body all disfigured and living the rest of his life knowing that could have been him. The horror had to have marked him in the ways I would be marked by Rodney King's brutalization when I was roughly the same age.

The Black families' collective decision to raise us all together was their best attempt to keep at bay the society that had murdered their heroes just a few years earlier. They deliberately constructed an idyllic childhood experience. And for a period in the mid-to-late 1980s, they were successful. Outside of trips to the 7-Eleven on Georgia Avenue, which was technically outside the neighborhood, I can't recall encountering the police growing up. And since we didn't see them, we didn't have to think about them. They simply weren't a part of our lives.

But even amid that success, a cloud of doom lingered. I graduated from sixth grade in 1987. That same school year Justice Antonin Scalia joined the Supreme Court. I know that Scalia is a hero to many of you reading this. I know you believe him to be a fair-minded, color-blind jurist of a conservative bent but who ultimately stuck to the law's original intent. I know you see him as a paragon of clarity, sobriety, and balance. But the Scalia that I know is the most dangerous kind of American precisely because of these noble characteristics. Consider two cases from his first year on the bench. In one, *McCleskey v. Kemp*, Scalia provided the fifth and decisive vote that sealed convicted murderer Warren McCleskey's death. The defense showed that Blacks were four times more likely to get the death penalty for killing whites than for killing Blacks in Georgia—that, essentially, white lives mattered more than Black lives. Despite this, in a memo to his colleagues, Scalia wrote that since racism is an "ineradicable" feature of US criminal legal process, there was no good reason to overturn McCleskey's death sentence.[11] By invoking a requirement to prove purposeful intent, *McCleskey* made it virtually impossible to win a racial discrimination suit against the criminal justice system.

This is where I struggle with certain white men. Your faith in our system of government can be so strong, so set, so fixed, that you willfully overlook the pain and suffering inflicted on your fellow citizens in order to uphold it. Your rule of law is so sacrosanct, your belief in this being a "government of laws not men" so sanctimonious, that you lose sight of the law's purpose—to prevent the persecution of a minority by the majority. Scalia's allegiance to color blindness and constitutional originalism was so strong that he intentionally and knowingly ignored an obvious injustice. *Yet you valorize this man.*

McCleskey coincided with the rise of the Drug War and colluded in the mass incarceration of Black men over the decades that have followed. As far back as 1987, observers regarded the decision as "the *Dred Scott*" decision of our time.[12] *McCleskey* was such a bad decision that the opinion's author, Lewis Powell, at the end of his life told his biographer that it was the single most regrettable ruling he had ever written while on the bench.[13] Scalia issued no such public admonition. Think about that. *Sit with that.*

And then reckon with the dissent Scalia wrote in *Johnson v. Transportation Agency* just a few months later—also in '87—first laying out what would become his signature argument against affirmative action. It's one that you may be familiar with. It goes something like this: "Black people have been wronged. No one disputes that. But we should only be in the business of using the law to remedy actual harms done to actual (Black) people.[14] We should not get into remedying past harms to 'even the score.' Victimizing 'innocent' white people who have nothing to do with racism today and elevating 'less qualified' Blacks into positions that, based on our objective measures of merit, they have not earned would denigrate our democracy."

This is a signature approach to racism taught in the

schools and universities I attended. It establishes that the speaker is not a racist, therefore the argument the speaker plans to present is not a product of racist views. It is a classic false moral conundrum that I find even well-meaning white people fall prey to. They acknowledge that we have a race problem that has created pervasive economic and social injustice in society. They say that they want more fairness and justice. They know that no amount of jobs programs or loan programs or college-access programs are ever going to close the economic divide that's grown between white people and Black people. But when it comes to fixing that problem, they get hung up on the idea of "set-aside programs" or "quotas." White people hear the word *reparations* and damn near blow a gasket. All of it amounts to the same thing. The thought of Black people possibly getting some recompense bothers white people. It gets under their skin. Even as it is clear wrongs have been done that whites would never want or tolerate, all sorts of rationalizations are put forward to keep the status quo intact. The threat of discrimination against a single white person gets equated with the fact of discrimination against an entire people.[15] A sober-minded concern with upholding meritocracy is stated even while white families with means do everything in their power to ensure that their children have and maintain self-fulfilling advantages from the beginning. The Fourteenth Amendment, a law born out of Reconstruction to ensure Black people could participate as citizens, is twisted into a means by which to protect white rights. This is the crux of color-blind racism.

What's ironic is that I get it.

My parents wanted me to have those same advantages. My parents extricated themselves from the dangers of the South and into middle-class D.C. For the first twelve years of my life they and the constellation of Black parents whose tables I ate at and floors I slept on and yards I played in sheltered me from the outside world. But, as my dad later told me when I asked why he had sent me to a school with white kids, D.C. was changing. Crack was already crawling its way through the hood. It was only a matter of time before it infiltrated Shepherd Park. Sidwell was a safe house where he could stash me until college. He was banking on the prevalence of white skin in the right zip code to protect my brown hue from harm. He was doing what he thought was right. He couldn't have known what was waiting for me once I walked through those doors.

Friend,

If I am honest, the things that stand out to me about my first days at Sidwell have little to do with school in the formal sense. I remember walking up the steps, through the glass entrance, and into what still strikes me as a grand atrium flooded with light. I was a huge Marvel Comics nerd at the time, so, to me, it felt as if I had entered Professor Xavier's School for Gifted Youngsters. If you recall, the diversity aim of the moment was a *melting pot*. It's one of the terms from the eighties and nineties, *tolerance* being another, that have since been discredited, abandoned,[16] and replaced with "woke" updates. But, for me, that I needed almost two hands to count the number of Black kids in my seventh-grade class was an unexpected early win. I remember watching my white classmates move through the halls with such ease and thinking that, like me, they were all of twelve yet seemed to know their destiny was to rule one day. I remember an early conversation wherein a classmate casually announced that he was going to an "Ivy" like his parents and thinking, (a) *What's an "Ivy"?* and (b) *How do you know something like that already?*

It didn't take long for me to start to draw some conclusions.

One of the first things I was told on my first day was

that my teachers were to be referred to by their first names. This was especially odd to me. Up to then, I'd only had one white teacher, Mrs. Powers. She was from the South and was only in D.C. because her husband got a big job in the Reagan administration. The rest of my teachers— from Ms. Robertson through Ms. Lassiter—were a carousel of Black women. They were all different. Robertson, with her soft lisp, was sweet. Jones was mean and strict. Lassiter let me know I was smart. Despite her bad hip, Loman pushed me relentlessly. They were all clearly authority figures, thus the formality of our relationship dictated I address them by their last names. At Sidwell, I went from raising my hand to use the bathroom to being on a first-name basis with all of my white teachers. Naturally, I thought I was hot shit. In the moment it felt like a simple Quaker school quirk. In retrospect, it strikes me as sending a powerful signal to a kid about their worth. The subtext was that we were equals. We were trusted. We mattered not as potential people but as currently existing, conscious human beings capable of making decisions.

The early revelations didn't stop. When I got my schedule, I noticed that I had a daily free period. The idea was so foreign to me that I had to ask a classmate what that even meant. That classmate chuckled because to them—to you—it was self-explanatory. *Free* meant "free." We could catch up on work. We could sit with a teacher to get additional help. We could goof off. We could wander campus. Notice how I used the word *wander*? It was intentional. No one *told* us what to do with our free period. That was entirely up to us. Again: subtext. Autonomy wasn't just a virtue, it was a value. It was core to our education. We were being educated on the wisdom of transcendental thinkers such as Ralph Waldo Emerson and his progressive-education descendant John Dewey. Our teachers were liberal white educators who saw in nature the solutions to modern materialism and a rebuke of the prosperity gospel that the industrial revolution had ushered in. Sidwell was, after all, a Quaker school. The antihierarchical, antimaterialistic ethos coursed through the design of our experience.

My seventh-grade social studies teacher, Saul, epitomized and embodied the school's ethos in the 1980s. He was an ex-hippie, and I wouldn't be surprised if he and Kurt, the art teacher, were sometimes stoned. Saul wore plaid shirts, ratty Levi's, and gnarly sneakers. He pulled his thinning mop in a ponytail some days. Others he just let his hair and bushy beard air-dry. Now that I recall, every morning Saul looked as if he hadn't finished drying off from a shower.

Getting Saul was a coup. Since he taught a mixed

seventh-and-eighth-grade class, being placed with him as a seventh grader meant the school thought you could hang with the older kids and with his college-lecturer approach. Rather than teach from the front of the class, Saul sat with us in a circle and led these mature discussions. The book I remember reading to this day—and still own a copy of—was Studs Terkel's *Working*. I didn't know what a leftist was and had never been to Chicago, but each day we'd read one or two of Studs's character portraits of working people and spend the rest of the time deconstructing language and meaning. Saul's class was more like a jam session than a lesson. Students offered their opinions and debated different interpretations, while Saul stroked his beard and considered every point we raised no matter how silly or clearly off the mark. At first, I just sat there mostly in silence, feeling intimidated by classmates who already seemed to know *how* to read deeply. This was all new to me—in my experience education had been rote memorization. The teacher formed questions that had a right or wrong answer. If you were right, you got rewarded. If you were wrong, you got humiliated. If you said something off-the-wall, Ms. Loman especially would look at you cock-eyed and ask if you were following the same lesson she was leading. Then she'd bawl you out. Kids crying in class was a regular thing. The potential for utter humiliation in front of your classmates was a motivating factor for me. Not at Sidwell. At Sidwell, everyone was sorta right even when obviously wrong, which even in my perpetual angst (Saul employed the Socratic method) I could decipher. Let's be honest, not all of us were geniuses. At Sidwell, you were rewarded for pontificating even when you didn't know what you were talking about or didn't have anything of substance to say. The key, what we were being taught, was to have an opinion and share it fearlessly.

Just one week into school, Saul announced the annual fall camping trip. He handed us a list of items we'd need, including a sleeping bag, tent, toiletries, and utensils. By then, I had watched the entire *Friday the 13th* oeuvre and had no interest whatsoever in a camping trip with white people. I was not about to be the Black kid knocked off at the beginning of the ax-murderer film. When I shared my misgivings with Saul the day after his announcement, he insisted the trip would be a way for me to bond with my classmates. So, reluctantly, I boarded our bus and took the two-hour ride to the middle of nowhere.

Saul was in his element. He led tent setup. He doled out commissary roles. He guided daytime hikes and organized nighttime campfires. In our downtime we were encouraged to sit and contemplate life. At the final night's closing campfire, I got up and freestyled. Thirty years later, I no longer know what compelled me to stand before my new classmates and rap about basketball, of all things. But what stands out to me was my innocence. Not only did it not occur to me that I was possibly performing a stereotype, I took the applause at face value. As cringe-inducing as that moment feels now, that little rap gained me a measure of popularity. Once back at school, kids I had never spoken to and who I didn't think knew I existed complimented me. Suddenly, I felt seen.

Once football season came around, my confidence surged. I might not have understood what white supremacy was or how it operated, but the Black-quarterback stigma wasn't lost on me.[17] I was determined to play quarterback, and sure enough, I earned the starting position. While we won only one game, the season stands out to me all these years later for other reasons. It was the first time that I traveled to suburban communities outside D.C. such as Bethesda and Potomac. We played on the perfectly manicured fields of schools called Landon, St. Stephens, Georgetown Prep, Bullis, and St. Albans—schools that formed my mental map when I later read coming-of-age novels such as *The Catcher in the Rye* and *A Separate Peace*. It was notable to me that each school had one or two (but no more) Black boys on their football team and, later, basketball teams. We—the Black boys on these otherwise all-white teams—were always the best or among the best players, and typically—but not exclusively—on some form of financial assistance. Initially, it felt as though we were pitted against one another. No matter which team we were playing, the game plan fixated on the other team's star Black guy. His body, his strength, and his speed were all topics of conversation. Naturally, as my team's star Black guy, I felt it was my duty to outperform my counterpart to prove my mettle. No one ever told us that this was the deal, but by virtue of our being flies in the ointment, we came to see one another as rivals vying for the title of top Black boy at the white-boy schools.

Is any of this news to you? Did it ever cross your mind that this competition for preeminence was happening all around you? Perhaps you did. Maybe you got a kick out of it. I can tell you that we didn't. For us Black boys, schadenfreude was the best way to describe our feelings toward one another. We all knew that our value and standing at our white school depended on our performance on the field of play. When we crossed paths at the rare, random social events for the Black kids who went to white schools, we tended to nod in acknowledgment but little else. In some perverse way, we were trained to despise one another. Only now, all these years later, have we discovered that we were part of an odd fraternity.

———

Friend,

It wasn't long before I started receiving invitations to hang out with my new classmates. I'm clear now in a way I wasn't then that I got those invites because I was a pretty good athlete. I know it sounds harsh, but it's important we speak truth to one another.

It's also true that I looked forward to those weekend getaways. They allowed me to pierce the otherwise invisible veil between in-school and out-of-school friendship. There, inside those homes, I started to notice the divide between white and Black D.C. My white friends lived west of Rock Creek Park, tucked inside a lush, secluded warren of mansions that I never even knew existed, in part because city planners, no doubt at the behest of influential homeowners, had resisted public transit plans in their communities, presumably to ward off the threat of crime and protect property values. It struck me that this side of our shared town was entirely white. All of the homeowners.

Everyone at the stores, in the restaurants, at the athletic club. I remember it occurring to me that your neighborhood operated completely separate and apart from the rest of D.C., my D.C. Why were the wealthiest neighborhoods in a majority-Black city exclusively white? Where were the Black people? As a kid, and without the context to understand the legacy of housing discrimination that I had been born into, I found this, more than anything else, just plain odd.

Roaming through the homes of my white friends was its own education. The homes that I grew up in were equally adorned with family photos, art, and books. But I was accustomed to Black faces smiling back at me, Black and African art in the halls, once-enslaved ancestors and freedom fighters on the walls, Black authors on the shelves, and Black music in the air. More than anything, though, those homes gave me a sense of purpose and pride, a connection to the broader Black diasporic family and the struggles we had endured and overcome. I never felt that sense of communal pride in the homes of my white friends. The art was awe inducing, but I hungered to learn something important about what my friends believed and how they felt about the world, yet I couldn't seem to penetrate beyond the surfaces surrounding me. I couldn't look at the photographs on the walls and gain a better understanding of where their people came from and what'd they gone through to get here. This isn't a judgment and I hope it doesn't come off that way. It was my experience. From what I saw, art, literature, music, even family, meant something different to you than to me. My parents needed to counteract America's chronic subordination of the Black experience. Outside our brief, sanitized studies of slavery, the Civil War, Jim Crow, and Civil Rights, we weren't taught about our journey in America, let alone in the world at large. Our parents' solution was to turn our homes into African American shrines, museums, and music halls. The parents of my white friends didn't have to instill their kids with a sense of white identity and self-esteem at home. The privilege of supremacy is silence. White superiority is ingrained in the unspoken ideology and institutional prerogatives that guide our lives. Therefore white parents were free—as in unchallenged—to express their individuality and unique sensibility, their personal aesthetic tastes and preferences if you will, without ever having to interrogate why, as freethinking people, most of the authors on their shelves and artists on their walls were white.

It didn't take long to begin noticing other silences in my

new world. Once a year we volunteered at a soup kitchen and women's shelter. At the kitchen, we served food to homeless men, most of whom were Black. At the shelter, we played with the small children of women who'd survived domestic abuse. Most were Black. I never questioned the character-enriching intention of these experiences. We were privileged young people being groomed to steward society; seeing injustice in our surroundings with our own eyes was important. But as well intended as those outings were, I worry that they did more harm than good. How is that so?

No one ever talked to us about the social and economic injustice that led to such hardships in the hood in the first place. None of us had any education on job discrimination, housing discrimination, the cycle of poverty, or the mental health crisis. No one told us that in the preceding years, Ronald Reagan had cut funding for low-income housing, jobs programs, and mental health institutions, all resulting in a massive rise in homelessness that he once had the temerity to say was by "choice."[18] In one stump speech after another, Reagan fabricated the fiction of the Black "welfare queen" stealing money from hardworking Americans. Even after journalists revealed the president's untruths, the stereotype of the profligate Black woman bearing too many children in order to milk the system endured for years to come and in many ways peaked with Bill Clinton's welfare-to-work legislation in 1997.

Against this uninformed backdrop, my classmates and I were sent into these downtrodden inner-city spaces to perform our obligatory community service. I hated these excursions. As a child, seeing my people in such a vulnerable and exposed condition in front of my classmates was embarrassing. I remember wanting to cover us up, close the door, turn off the lights. This was family business.

What was more, once the ordeal was finally over, we returned to the Sidwell bubble to resume our lives without ever being challenged to consider why so many Black people in our city were in such straits two decades after the movement that supposedly brought equality. Nor were we challenged to ask why in a majority-Black city so few of our teachers were Black. After elementary school I didn't have a single Black female educator until college. They were all either white (women and men) or the occasional Black male. In stark contrast, the subservient roles on campus were staffed exclusively by people of color. Black women served us lunch. Black men policed the campus. El Salvadoran men kept the grounds neat.

Does any of this feel familiar to your own experience? Was your formative exposure to Black people similarly limited? If so, what ideas about the Black community started to form as a result? Have you ever wondered whether the absence of Black women—any women of color—conditioned you to devalue their labor? To question their authority? To doubt their expertise? Can you see how, in the absence of clarity and context, we might have drawn racist conclusions and formed racist beliefs about the roles white people and Black people are supposed to play?

As I look back, what troubles me deeply about these community service excursions is that while I was trained to perform painfully close readings of the *Iliad* and analyze the hell out of Shakespeare's verses, my education did not teach me to notice, name, and make meaning of the bizarre racial schisms right before our eyes. Inasmuch as we valued intellectual discourse in the abstract—debate—no one pushed us to grapple critically with the great discord in our midst. So we came to believe charity was the extent of our responsibility. Give to good causes and practice politeness to those beneath us. But there is a great distance between politeness and justice. A just education wouldn't have been satisfied with representational diversity among the children. A just education would have demanded more Black faculty not only for the Black kids but for everybody.

The silences around race penetrated the classrooms as

well. When it was discussed, slavery was referred to euphemistically as the "peculiar institution." Crispus Attucks was an American patriot because he died for American liberty. Meanwhile, Nat Turner and Denmark Vesey were radicals and extremists because they were willing to kill for Black freedom. We learned plenty about the "antebellum" period and the Civil War, but I didn't encounter the promise and peril of Reconstruction until I started studying history on my own after college. In eighth grade we read *Othello* in English class. That same year, five Black boys in New York City were accused of raping a white woman in Central Park, while in Boston a white man accused a fictional Black man of killing his pregnant wife. I remember encountering the headlines and news coverage of both incidents as we were working our way through the play. To me, the messaging was crystal clear: Black men were sexual predators who preyed on white women. We were not to be trusted. Yet, even though I was the only Black boy in a class full of white girls, none of this was ever touched upon. I was left to reckon on my own.

It only got worse from there. With each book we read—*The Great Gatsby, The Catcher in the Rye, To Kill a Mockingbird*—the casual racism cut me a little deeper. How could these be held up as great texts yet be so matter-of-factly racist? I didn't understand. Nor, clearly, did my teachers. They could have said this is not right and is a failure of the text and, perhaps, the author as well, but they didn't. This was great American literature and our job was to learn why, not to question that assertion. Thus, each time we breezed over a passage without pausing to process and make sense, I found myself disengaging. It became my way of getting through. I was no more prepared or interested in having those conversations than my classmates, but given my race, I would have to reckon someday soon with the attitudes we told ourselves had disappeared but clearly hadn't.

————

Although silence was smothering the race conversation in and around my formal education, race was becoming an ever-more-present feature of my life outside school. At the start of eighth grade, I joined one of the top traveling basketball teams in the city. After school each day, I took two buses across town and entered a raucous boys' club gym for practice. The Kingman Pythons were the pride of Columbia Heights, a neighborhood that had yet to recover from the riots following Martin Luther King's death and was now being infiltrated by crack cocaine. Most of the boys on my team attended local public schools and lived in either one of the deteriorating apartment buildings or pre-gentrified row houses dotting the neighborhood.

My new teammates didn't accept me, at least not initially. At Sidwell, I was an outsider because I was neither rich nor white. With these boys and in that neighborhood, I was an outsider because I lived uptown and attended a lily-white private school. My teammates rode me hard in practice and teased me relentlessly on the rides to and from our games. At first, I took it personally and even thought about quitting. I felt unfairly targeted. I didn't decide where we lived. It wasn't my fault that my dad sent me to private school. Then it occurred to me that, aside from one or two dads who showed up here and there, the fathers of my teammates weren't around. They never mentioned their whereabouts either. Our coaches—Hitch, Ruck, and Larry—were the men who made sure their players ate dinner, got home safely, and did their schoolwork and stayed out of trouble.

Over time, I began to understand that my claims of innocence were irrelevant. My desire for my teammates to see me as an individual—just as one of the guys—was about *my* discomfort with feeling the discomfort that they lived in daily. They knew that they were being shortchanged in their schools and neighborhoods. I ventured into the hood to play basketball, but once practice ended, I returned to my cozy neighborhood where a full fridge, backyard hoop, and my own bedroom awaited. So, of course, they wanted to destroy me on the court. I had to learn to accept their contempt and not take it personally because it wasn't about me. It was about the situation. As I came to understand the terms of the arrangement, that if I was going to enter their world, I had to adjust to their norms, they began to accept me. I became part of the group.

In my experience, the white boys who are able to successfully navigate Black cultural spaces learn a similar lesson. They come to understand that they are guests. They don't make the rules. They don't get to be defensive or uptight. They either laugh at the jokes and understand that that's just a small sample of the indignities Black people endure, or they leave.

As that basketball season in those two very different worlds wore on, I began to notice other differences. At Sidwell, practice was structured around set plays—we had a play for everything. Our style emphasized crisp bounce passes, hard screens, minimal dribbling or one-on-one action, and bank shots off the glass. Any sign of playground ball gave our coaches an ulcer. "Run the offense," they barked rigidly from the sidelines. If I didn't follow their directives, they sat me on the bench. Even after I made a slick move I'd honed at Shepherd playground and scored, they'd fold their arms and purse their lips. But if one of the white players dove for a loose ball, took a charge, or made what was considered a "heady" play, the coaches would order the entire team to clap it up.

At the boys' club, we ran laps and sprints until we couldn't see straight. We ran drills with a medicine ball. We weight trained. We went over plays countless times. But once the ball was tipped, we were trusted to play. If I could take my defender, I had that freedom. "Play *your* game," my coaches whispered encouragingly if they ever thought I was hesitating or overthinking. In that way, they taught me to trust myself—the exact opposite of what I was learning to do across town.

At fourteen, I didn't have the lens or language to name what I was experiencing in these Black and white D.C. worlds. Because I wanted to play, I never openly challenged the authority of my white coaches. I just knew that I often felt something was off. Without the boys' club world, I would have thought it was me. I would have assumed that I needed to learn how to fit into a system that clearly wasn't designed for someone such as me. Instead, my need to reconcile that dissonance I was feeling internally led me to take note of other inconsistencies. I began picking up on the coded language that sports commentators used during televised basketball games. White analysts especially—Billy Packer comes to mind—praised the intellect ("What a heady play") and moral character ("He's a hard worker") of white players. Black players rarely received that praise. We were "naturals." We had physical gifts. We could run and jump. That was our value, and that went unexamined.

The NCAA passed a controversial eligibility requirement called Proposal 42, or Prop 42, that season. The rule required all incoming student athletes to have a minimum GPA and SAT/ACT score to receive an athletic scholarship from a Division I school. Even though everyone knew the rule was going to disproportionately impact Black athletes, it was framed by its proponents as a race-neutral policy that upheld the integrity of collegiate athletics. In this way, Prop 42 exemplified the emerging color-blind approach to policy making that the Supreme Court first established in 1976's *Washington v. Davis*.[19]

I wouldn't have thought twice about Prop 42 were it not for Georgetown University basketball coach John Thompson. At the time, "Big John," as he was known in D.C., was the most visible and successful Black coach in America. He was the first Black coach to win an NCAA men's basketball title and coach a USA Olympic team. He'd sent at least a dozen players to the NBA. Thompson was also six feet ten inches, dark skinned, and unapologetic. After the rule was passed, Thompson used his clout to call out the SAT as culturally biased. He further charged Prop 42 with unfairly targeting athletes from low socioeconomic backgrounds.

He didn't stop there.

Just before tip time of Georgetown's nationally televised game against Boston College on the eve of Martin Luther King Day, Thompson draped his signature towel over his assistant's shoulder and walked off the court. He boycotted the game in protest. The crowd at the old Capital Centre rose to its feet. A week later, the NCAA announced that it was pausing the rule.

In Prop 42's wake, some praised Thompson. Others criticized his stance as narrow-minded, a term often used to belittle and discredit Black thinking or the centering of Black narratives.[20] Notwithstanding the chance he took on Allen Iverson after Virginia's first Black governor, Douglas Wilder, pardoned him from a fifteen-year sentence for allegedly instigating a bowling alley brawl, none of Thompson's accomplishments compared to his Prop 42 protest. In retrospect, it was the first Black protest that felt relevant to my experience.

———

Friend,

My next awakening hit closer to home. When I first arrived at Sidwell, I was placed in remedial math. No one called it that, but that's what it was. I'd been in advanced math classes so it was somewhat of a sting to my pride. I begged my parents to get me out of the class, so they scheduled a meeting with my teacher, who explained that I didn't need to worry. The class was just meant to smooth my transition. If all went well, I'd be placed in the grade-level math class the following year. I put my head down and powered through.

The next year I was placed in pre-algebra with the majority of my classmates. I wasn't the best student, but I held my own. Yet, at the end of the year my teacher pulled me aside to say that she wasn't advancing me to algebra. I hadn't mastered the material to her satisfaction. Once again, my parents came to the school. After some discussion, a compromise was reached. I could advance to algebra provided I passed a special test at the end of the summer.

To prepare me, my parents hired a math professor at Howard University to be my summer tutor. At our first meeting, the professor, a serious man with a strong Caribbean accent who wore an even stronger sandalwood-scented cologne, handed me a quiz and walked away.

"Come and find me when you are finished," he said, closing the door behind him.

After I finished the quiz, I sought him out. Without acknowledging me, the professor donned his glasses and began grading my work. I watched him scribble notes and comments. Then he added up the score, removed his glasses, and locked his eyes with me. I in turn glanced down at the paper.

"Remind me, why are you here?" he asked, handing me a near-perfect score.

My tutor's question swirled around in my head all summer long. Those six words affirmed both what I already knew and didn't want to know. I wasn't crazy or dumb. I knew the material just fine. What I hadn't wanted to know was that my teacher—an otherwise well-intentioned woman with whom I had gone on camping and community service trips for two years—had decided to play gatekeeper.

She and she alone had decided that I was simply not ready for the rigors that awaited, therefore it was in *my* best interest to repeat a class I had already passed.

This was my first direct encounter with the color-blind meritocracy mythos that was taking hold of both liberal and conservative ideology, though certainly not my last. Three years later, my eleventh-grade physics teacher made the same judgment call when he decided, in his little office and without consulting anyone, that he wasn't allowing me to advance to advanced biology, effectively ending my formal science education.

I had been taught to believe, as I'm sure you were as well, that doing well and scoring well was all that mattered. The test, we were drilled into believing, was the great equalizer. Up to then I had never considered that the warmhearted, liberal-minded adults I was being educated by might still hold such base biases or harbor such paternalistic convictions. It wouldn't surprise me in the least to hear you say that you never encountered prejudice in your educational experience. Nor would it surprise me if you were to advise me, as a friend, to remain reasonable. To not blow one or two arguably discriminatory experiences with a couple of teachers out of proportion.

The reality is that my one experience was not an

anomaly. Recent peer-reviewed studies have shown that teachers hold the same pro-white biases as Americans at large.[21] It's also been empirically demonstrated that white teachers have lower expectations for Black students and are less likely to enroll them in advanced-placement classes.[22] And here's the kicker: the Black-white achievement gap persists across class and even in affluent suburban school districts.[23] The upshot: Black people can't even buy their way out of bias.

Given this context, when you look back on your education, how many Black students can you count in your classes? I could be wrong, but my guess is that even if we were in the same building, we were on a different academic track. Did you ever ask yourself why? Did you just assume that we didn't want to be in advanced-placement classes? That we weren't applying ourselves? Or did you just not even think about it?

At minimum, consider this. Your humanity—literally whether you are actually human or not—has never been the subject of debate. The Supreme Court never said that you had no rights that needed to be respected. Science never argued that your brain was smaller to prove you were less intelligent. Your subjugation was never rationalized by myths and stereotypes about your unbridled aggression and shiftless indolence. In short, you didn't need to develop an independent understanding of the world and your place in it in order to remain intact.

―――――

Friend,

I aced the end-of-summer math test. Then I aced the first few quizzes and tests to start the school year.

I was just starting to feel good about myself when a classmate approached me in the hallway one day and asked if it was true.

"Is what true?"

"You know . . ."

I'd naively shared my grades with one of our classmates, who, in turn, shared it with others, until the news made it back to me in the form of a question that explained why more than a few of our classmates kept staring me in the hallway. They all knew.

"*How* did you do it?" my inquisitor asked.

". . . I studied?" I answered, wondering where this was headed.

Judging by my classmate's stiff gaze, I had broken an unspoken covenant. We could be buddies. It was perfectly fine for me to outplay him on the court. But I wasn't supposed to outperform him in the classroom. That was his domain.

When I think about the harm that white supremacy does to white children, two distinct moments from my youth always come to mind. The first: During a game of tag on a school bus in second grade, I reached out to tag a classmate. Before my fingers could even graze her skin, she shot me a look so lethal I instinctually jumped back. "Don't put your Black hands on me," she said just as calmly as Sunday morning on Main Street. I had been in school with this girl for three years. She had always struck me as friendly. Every ounce of warmth I had felt for her drained out of me in that moment.

The hallway encounter above is the second. There's a famous scene from *Do the Right Thing* when Mookie interrogates Vito, who uncompunctiously considers all Black people not named Prince, Magic Johnson, and Eddie Murphy niggers. What's so fascinating and brilliantly captured in that scene is Vito's certainty. He doesn't even think for an instant that he is wrong. He simply doesn't question it. That's what the hallway encounter felt like for me. Quite clearly, everything my so-called friend had seen, heard, and learned about Black people had so thoroughly convinced him of my genetic inferiority that he refused to process the possibility that he had been sold a false bill of goods.

But, again, it all makes sense when you think about it. Outside the bubble that was Black D.C., official Washington—the seat of national power and global politics—was run exclusively by white men. The news anchors, public intellectuals, judges, lawyers, doctors, teachers, architects, designers, creators, authors. Basically, anybody who had any authority was white. Even the imaginary world beamed into our homes was all-white. Consider our generation's prime-time television options: *The Dukes of Hazzard, Dallas, Dynasty, Falcon Crest, Charlie's Angels, Wonder Woman, The Six Million Dollar Man, The Love Boat, Fantasy Island, The A-Team, MacGyver, Magnum P.I., Diff'rent Strokes, Starsky & Hutch,* and on and on. Isaac, Mr. T, and Benson notwithstanding, can you recall a single Black lead? How about a Black woman lead? The entire entertainment industrial complex that we were raised in centered white male leads. They solved the mysteries. They won the battles; saved society; got the girl; had the money, power, and respect. They had the brains. They were moral. They were kind. They were sincere. They were brave. They were everywhere and everything—so ubiquitous that their dominance was hidden in plain sight.

How could this not influence us? You in one way, me in another.

That hallway exchange signaled a turning point. I didn't know it, but middle school had marked the end of innocence. The stakes were real now. Lines had been drawn. After that, I knew that I posed a threat to an unspoken, established order. In the eyes of my classmates, I had a fixed identity. I was a diversity kid who played basketball. I was only in school with them because of affirmative action. The idea that I might be more than that stereotype would have required them to reconsider the world as they were comfortable seeing it. They were neither prepared nor motivated to do that. Our little world had already made abundantly clear what mattered and how to attain it. "Western civ" was mandatory. Black history was an elective. *Beowulf* was a requirement. Baldwin was an elective. Think about that. I had to learn the history and culture of white people. That experience was considered universal. Compounding matters, our education didn't even attempt to unearth and challenge any racist ideas we, myself included, may have harbored. It, instead, handed us a cheat sheet with key figures and dates. It told us who the good guys and the bad guys were and even how to identify them. White supremacists smoked cigars, had big bellies and sweaty necks, and wore big-brimmed hats. The worst of them wore white caps and burned crosses in the woods. As long as you weren't one of *them*, you were presumed to be one of the good guys.

The rest of high school was a slog. Surrounded as I felt by peers who didn't seem to harbor similar inner doubts about their place in the world made me wonder if my class-mate was right to ask how someone who was possibly only at Sidwell because the standards had been lowered could outperform him. Every test, paper, and classroom discussion became an assessment of our collective Black worth. Consequently, I hid behind a veil of performative indifference. Even if I knew the answer to questions, I remained quiet. The pressure to be perfect felt too heavy. Every time I opened my mouth I felt I had to prove that I wasn't there to fill a quota. I later learned that this was a signature feature of "stereotype threat."[24] It was a Sisyphean task. Even when I did well, I brushed off my performance as luck, which I have come to identify as a feature of racial impostor syndrome.[25] I was left to wonder if my teacher had gone easy on me. If I didn't do well, I saw it as confirmation that I didn't belong. Holding all of that was cognitively taxing, and I, admittedly, wasn't always up to that task.[26]

There's a saying attributed to Martin Luther King that

eleven o'clock on Sunday morning is the most segregated hour in America. Once high school began, I observed that my white classmates led a totally separate social life from mine between 3:00 P.M. on Friday and 8:00 A.M. on Monday. That other life included their counterparts at nearby prep schools but, for the most part, excluded Black students. I only knew it existed because I heard the whispers between periods about who got wasted and who hooked up at the kegger. When I did have the audacity to show up uninvited, I knew right away that I was not welcome. The same people I went to school with Monday through Friday acted as if they didn't know who I was on Saturday. I may as well have been the wallpaper. The message was plain: I wasn't welcome.

My growing disillusionment coincided with the Clarence Thomas hearings. Two years after that hallway exchange, George H. W. Bush nominated Thomas to replace Thurgood Marshall on the Supreme Court. The nomination stands out as a prime example of white men tokenizing Black people and thereby diminishing us all. Thomas's nomination was opposed by the NAACP, AFL-CIO, and many more groups because of his record at the Equal Employment Opportunity Commission (EEOC) and, despite its obvious benefits to his own life, his vocal opposition to affirmative action.[27]

In my household and in most Black households I spent time in, Thomas's nomination was a total repudiation of everything Justice Marshall stood for. Despite Bush's assurances that Thomas was the best qualified candidate—that, in other words, he merited the job—Black people knew that job opening would have been filled by another white man had any justice other than Marshall retired. We knew then as we know now that two Black people—even two with polar opposite views—sitting on the nation's highest bench together is still an unreal proposition for white people. There are a couple of reasons for this. On one hand, inasmuch as white people pride themselves on their individuality, Black people are still largely regarded as a monolith. Our need to gather as a minoritized group to protect one another and survive intact has been twisted to mean we are all one and the same. And if we all think alike, why would we need two of us on the bench when one will do? On the other hand, the presence of too many Black people in any space other than those that have been defined as "Black" creates discomfort for white people. There is at once a worry, a likely holdover from slavery, that we will cook up an insurrection, and a concern that too many of us diminishes the value of said space.

Even if you don't quite buy my assertions about Bush's

true motivations in nominating Thomas, what's indisputable is that just two months earlier he sent the graduating class at Michigan off into the world with the following message:

"The notion of political correctness has ignited controversy across the land. And although the movement arises from the laudable desire to sweep away the debris of racism and sexism and hatred, it replaces old prejudice with new ones. It declares certain topics off-limits, certain expression off-limits, even certain gestures off-limits."

There is just so much to unpack in these three sentences. For starters, Michigan would soon emerge as a key battleground in the fight to end affirmative action. For another, Bush delivered this speech a mere two months after the Rodney King video first aired. Why he decided that was the right moment to suggest that the "debris of racism" was all that remained is beyond me. I also want to call attention to two ideas baked into the sentences above that, I think, disserved our generation. The first: prejudice and racism were one and the same. This false equivalency simplified our thinking about a complex problem with deep historical roots. The second: American values were being attacked by "political correctness." The entire notion was woven out of whole cloth. The struggle for equity and inclusion was never about silencing or taking anything from white people. It was about justice for identities and experiences that had been marginalized by racism.

Political correctness, meanwhile, was the brainchild of Allan Bloom's 1987 book, *The Closing of the American Mind.* In it, Bloom ridiculed the new educational zeitgeist that had replaced Western reason with multicultural mumbo jumbo, lamented the lost days when college students "actually knew something about and loved England, France, Germany or Italy," and belittled the current generation's growing interest in "the political problems of Third World countries." Bloom charitably praised white students, whom he felt had transcended even being "subtly racist" for their willingness to "talk themselves into accepting affirmative action." But his observations of Black students—a group he literally referred to as "peculiar"—require particular attention. Even though discriminatory laws were now "ancient history," Bloom was irked that Black students would not "melt as have all other groups." His contempt was clear. It simply wasn't enough that Black people had been admitted to elite schools that they hadn't earned the right to attend. They had the temerity to intimidate administrators into adding Black "enrichment courses" and demand the hiring of Black faculty.

The Closing of the American Mind became a wildly popular bestseller. It sold a half million *hardback* copies. Just as our generation was coming of age, Bloom's sentiments emerged as the new contrarian consensus. His ideas were considered bold, courageous. He was valorized for telling hard truths.

Tell me, who do you think were among the book's purchasers? I can assure you that it wasn't on my bookshelf at home. Nor was Bloom quoted at my dinner table.

The people who bought Bloom's book were our teachers and professors. CEOs bought the book. Pundits. Legislators. By and by, its ideas made their way into the Oval Office and back out to our generation as virtue. And I'm willing to bet that none of Bloom's acolytes thought they were racist. They were just realists. People dealing with the world as it presented itself to them.

If we're going to keep it real with one another, let me level with you: Clarence Thomas's nomination was never for or about Black people. Thurgood Marshall's nomination in the summer of '67, when the country was in flames, was for and about Black people. George Bush pushed Clarence Thomas forward for white people—for *you.* It was an appeal to *your* color-blind values. It was intended to show that America had come so far since the 1960s that even a

Black conservative could sit on the highest bench. It didn't matter that Thomas's views represented a pitiful fraction of the Black population to which he owed his nomination. It didn't matter that a Black woman risked her reputation and livelihood to tell the world he had made unwelcome sexual advances toward her. It didn't even matter that Black people said that he was unqualified based on the standards of merit white people swear allegiance to and fret that affirmative action ultimately undermines. It only mattered that white men could proudly tell one another that race relations were improving, which, ironically, is precisely why Justice Thomas abhors affirmative action.[28]

Clarence Thomas's confirmation came at a steep political price for Bush. He hadn't factored in Anita Hill or that her testimony would spark widespread outrage even among white women who identified with her experience in male-dominated spaces. To make immediate amends, Bush signed the 1991 Civil Rights Act one month after Thomas's confirmation. The law was the first major renovation of the 1960s legislation and a basic reprise of a bill that Bush, who opposed the 1964 civil rights law in a failed US House campaign, vetoed a year earlier. The new and improved law also imposed hefty fines on employers shown to discriminate on the basis of race or gender. By tightening employment discrimination laws that had been loosened in the preceding years by the Supreme Court, the 1991 law was supposed to, finally, open up jobs and industries that white men continued to dominate. Republicans called it a "quota" bill and worried that the threat of litigation and hefty fines for violators would lead to reverse discrimination, a bogeyman universally proclaimed and rarely born out.

Well, you can probably guess what actually happened. Corporate America simply avoided hiring Black people. A 2003 study tracking the effect of those fears in real terms found that Black employment and hours worked "dropped relative to whites starting in 1992."[29] Also in 1991, the Supreme Court upheld the first mandatory arbitration agreement barring an employee from filing civil rights lawsuits. The upshot: Facing a moral reckoning that could have led to economic justice, the white men in charge chose their interests in avoiding legal blowback over our collective interest in building an equitable society. Just as Gen Xers—the first generation born into the new social experiment— were entering the workforce, Black people were being quietly and systematically shut out and up, this time under the aegis of corporate protectionism. The Economic Policy

Institute now estimates that sixty million American workers are now under arbitration agreements.[30]

Even a civil rights Hail Mary couldn't save George Bush's presidency. When Bill Clinton made him a member of the one-term club in 1992, the experts said the recession, Ross Perot, and the whole "no new taxes" backtrack cost him his job. But if you look at the demographic exit poll data from 1988[31] and 1992,[32] something else stands out. In '88 and again in '92, women accounted for 52 percent and 53 percent of the vote respectively. In '88, Bush won women by 2 percent. In 1992, he lost them by 7 percent—a 9-point swing. Notably, Bush lost to Clinton by 6 percent.

———

Friend,

At the start of senior year, I was being recruited by a handful of smaller Division I schools. Under NCAA rules, athletic prospects could accept a limited number of campus-visit invitations. I took one of mine with another Black player who attended a school in the same conference as Sidwell.

The campus was tucked in the Lehigh Valley. Upon our

arrival, an assistant coach and a pair of players gave us the grand tour. We walked the campus and shot hoops in the gym. We ate in the cafeteria and attended a class. At night, the players brought us to a frat party. Wherever we went, people greeted us warmly and encouraged us to attend. We would love it here, they said, and we both smiled in exchange.

Back at our hotel, the two of us stayed up late talking. In all the years we'd competed against each other, we'd never gotten to know each other. That night we did. Our experiences as Black boys in white spaces were eerily alike. It was refreshing to talk with someone who understood exactly what I was experiencing.

"Can you see yourself here?" I asked him.

The coaches were selling us the idea of being the building blocks of the future. It was flattering and exciting. We started to imagine ourselves playing together.

"Tell me something. Did you see even a single Black student on campus who wasn't on the basketball team?"

"Come to think of it, I didn't," I said. "Do you think that's why they want us?"

"They want *us* because they already know we can hack it."

It dawned on me then that I didn't want to "hack it"

through college. I couldn't. I needed college to be something different. The next morning we told the coaches thanks but no thanks. Then we boarded a train back to D.C.

As I look back, that conversation seems like a luxury. Basketball or not, I was going to college. Sidwell had given me that certainty. But while my classmates were applying to the top schools in America, my top criteria were getting out of a D.C. that had become increasingly dangerous for Black boys, and being around Black people.

Rutgers checked both boxes, plus the basketball coach promised me a preferred tryout. But then classes began and something unexpected happened. I did well. My professors started pulling me aside to tell me that I showed promise. The encouragement made me hungrier. Suddenly, I was a student again. Not only that, I found a crew of Black friends. They came from Newark, East Orange, Passaic, and Trenton, yet they accepted this D.C. kid without reservation. On top of all that, I was surrounded by beautiful Black women. And unlike the girls at Sidwell, they actually noticed me. When tryouts rolled around, I told the coach thanks but no thanks.

Friend,

My college experience would likely have started and finished uneventfully if it hadn't been for Charles Murray's 1994 book, *The Bell Curve.* I would have done well, earned my degree, and gone on to grad school or into the workplace. Like so many in my generation, I would have looked back on my college years as the best four years of my life and little more. We weren't in the midst of an unpopular war. The economy under Bill Clinton was growing. The dot-com era was just getting underway, and the future of tech seemed both boundless and bias-free. Overall, the mid-nineties were an optimistic moment, especially for young people such as me who didn't consider themselves political.

The Bell Curve did appear, however, just as my second year at Rutgers started. Murray's book claimed to offer irrefutable scientific evidence that Black people had lower IQs than whites and Asians. Because IQ is mostly genetic and therefore unchangeable, Murray and his coauthor, Richard Herrnstein (who died shortly after publication), asserted that investing in programs such as affirmative action, Head Start, and even welfare was a waste of public resources. *Newsweek, The New Republic, Time, The New York Times, The New York Times Magazine, The New York*

Times Book Review, The Wall Street Journal, Forbes, National Review—they and many others ran major features on and reviews of the book. The major networks covered it. Pundits offered opinions about it. And while many of these prominent outlets and opinionators criticized the book, that was beside the point. The most respected media outfits in our republic gave racism a platform to have its case heard.

I want you to just think about that for a moment. These publications would never have allowed bogus ideas about people of Jewish descent to be presented to the public as science. It would have been a public outrage. People would have lost their jobs. Careers would have been ruined. Yet, white-owned, mainstream media allowed this to happen to Black people, and at least initially everyone went along for the ride.

The publication was met with widespread criticism in the scientific community, and in the months after publication it was revealed that its authors had lacked training as geneticists.[33]

The Human Genome Project, The National Academy of Sciences, and the American Psychological Association all denounced the book as crank science. The NAS conducted its own independent review of the data and concluded that much of it was wrong, its analysis flawed, and its conclusions erroneous.

In fact, it was reported that Murray and Herrnstein did not submit their work for peer review, something traditionally done with scientific works. Murray once even told a *New York Times Magazine* reporter, "[s]ome of the things we read to do this work, we literally had to hide when we're on planes and trains."[34]

The authors also carefully buried the shady sources upon which their biased thesis and shoddy data relied in footnotes they knew few would research. These included studies conducted by known eugenicists, white supremacists and outright racists whose work had been funded by the Pioneer Fund, a white supremacist foundation whose founder believed the United States should exterminate its Black population. If you are starting to feel nauseous, hold on to your stomach; there's more.

Murray's million-dollar research and media blitz was backed entirely by the conservative Bradley Foundation. The foundation also funded Murray's fellowship at the American Enterprise Institute.

Why is all of this important? In one sense, like me, you probably didn't read the book. Yet, you were undoubtedly exposed to its ideas. Those ideas were presented to us as science when in fact they were pure propaganda. Although a full-on campaign to debunk the book ensued shortly after its publication, it was like cleaning up an oil spill. No amount of damage control could undo the harm the book had done.

That harm hit home for me in the spring of my sophomore year. In 1995, on January 31—Black History Month eve—*The Newark Star-Ledger* published a recorded statement in which Rutgers University president Francis Lawrence said that Black students lacked the "genetic, hereditary background to have a higher average" on standardized tests. Lawrence had made the remarks during a faculty meeting the previous November. Notably, no one in the meeting spoke up at the time.

My initial reaction was to ignore the story. To me, it wasn't a coincidence that the news had leaked the day before Black History Month. Clearly, someone was using Black students to carry out their agenda. Moreover, upon further review, the broader context in which Lawrence made the remarks indicated that he was concerned with setting test-based standards that excluded Black students.

My Black friends didn't see it that way. They started calling meetings to discuss collective-action options. I, meanwhile, called my dad, who told me to keep my head down and stay out of trouble. Do your work, he said, and let that be your response. I trusted Dad so I listened.

Even after the protests started and more of my friends began getting involved, I continued going to class and minding my business. Then, in the midst of the first sold-out basketball game at Rutgers in three years, against Massachusetts, then the number two-ranked basketball team in the country, a student walked onto the court at halftime and sat down. Other students left the stands and joined her. The game had to be postponed.

ESPN was on campus the next day. Jesse Jackson showed up shortly thereafter. For his part, Lawrence defended his record of supporting college access for students of color and apologized to whoever would listen. He said his remarks were "stupid" and "foolish." But in a *New York Times* story he finally revealed what had been on his mind:

"When Mr. Lawrence ponders his comments, he said he probably made them because he had been thinking and talking about reviews of *The Bell Curve*, a book that examines the links between genetics and intellectual achievement."[35]

Through it all, I remained disengaged, until one day while returning from my work-study gig I crossed paths with a group of friends on their way to a march. On a whim, I joined them. We boarded a bus to College Avenue and merged into a gathering crowd inside Voorhees Mall. After student leaders spoke, hundreds of us marched through New Brunswick and onto Route 18, where we shut down traffic in both directions. News choppers arrived. Police descended. Once we arrived at President Lawrence's home, we stood in his driveway demanding his resignation. When we learned that he wasn't even there, we dispersed.

The next day I returned to class. But when I arrived at my dorm that evening, a summons from the New Brunswick Police Department was under my door. I had been charged with reckless endangerment.

I quickly learned that out of the hundreds of protesters who took over the highway, only two others had been charged by the NBPD. Both were Black males like me. I knew them through the intramural basketball league, but I wasn't even with them that day so I found it baffling that the three of us were the only ones charged.

I spent the spring trying to make sense of what had happened that day. Why I was singled out. Why all of my friends were allowed to move on with their lives without consequence while I, a dilettante, was left to face punishment. My grades plummeted. My girlfriend broke up with me. I fell into a depression. To cope, I turned to alcohol, weed, and dark rap. I was lost.

In the thick of summer, Dad drove me back to New Jersey to stand trial. We didn't speak the whole ride up. I was too ashamed and he was too disappointed. I recall walking into the courtroom with him by my side, then up to the bench alone to face the judge and prosecutor. I felt so vulnerable and at the mercy of a system that had the power to snatch me up. It took me standing before the judge to realize that I honestly hadn't thought President Lawrence's remarks applied to me. I had done relatively well on the SAT. I had a strong GPA. Yet, none of that had protected me.

Because I was a first-time offender and a student, I got off with community service. As long as I fulfilled the terms, the charges would be dropped. Once I had my paperwork, my father and I headed back to D.C. I spent the ride examining the thinking that had led me to ignore the protests. As I did, more hidden truths emerged.

I hadn't *only* ignored the protests because I thought Lawrence's remarks were aimed elsewhere. I saw myself as different from the other Black students. I considered myself exempt because of my experiences in an elite white school. I thought because I had gone to school with the children of powerful white people, I was one of them.

It didn't take long for me to start to see the other judgments that I was making on that foundational belief of my exemption. My Black friends didn't work as hard. They weren't as hungry. Maybe if they applied themselves, they would do better. It never occurred to me that at the heart of it all my fellow Black students felt betrayed and hurt by the school. For many of them, just getting to college had been an achievement. They'd overcome major obstacles, defied stereotypes, and broken family barriers only for the president of the university to which they'd tied their futures to say they were genetically inferior. I felt ashamed for my callousness. My friends were in pain. They felt mistreated, and all I had done was sit in silent judgment.

I joined the Black and Latino student newspaper the next school year. I started off writing music reviews and graduated to features. I also joined a consciousness-raising study group and spent Saturday nights discussing such texts as *Wretched of the Earth, How Capitalism Underdeveloped Black America, Soul on Ice, Blood in My Eye, The Spook Who Sat by the Door, To Kill a Black Man, The COINTEL-PRO Papers, Black Bourgeoisie,* and *The Mis-Education of the Negro.* I carried Assata Shakur's autobiography around like a sacred text. I discovered James Baldwin's *No Name in the Street* and learned about Martin Luther King's Poor

People's Campaign in Chicago. I found W. E. B. Du Bois, Howard Zinn, Noam Chomsky, Marx and Engels, Che Guevara. My mind was blown.

When I first encountered the shadow history of Black revolutionary struggle, I longed to be part of it. It offered me a noble story of my people's relentless quest for liberation and the white power structure's unbending resistance to change. But to immerse myself in that tradition, I had to reconcile my personal history. I was a child of the Black bourgeoisie that had benefited from the movement and, by some accounts, left poor Blacks behind. This Black middle class moved to suburbs and sent its children to private schools. It held debutante balls and organized exclusive social groups such as Jack and Jill. It summered in Martha's Vineyard and Sag Harbor. It valued light skin over dark. Too often its pretentiousness mimicked elite white standards of achievement. I was a part of that. That was a part of me.

Just as the moment of racial injustice after George Floyd's murder disturbed your sense of things, that period of reckoning in my life unsettled me. It forced me to ask myself if I was an accomplice to the oppressive system that trapped so many Black bodies in the cycle of poverty and prison. I first had to accept that I directly benefited from the struggle that generations of Black folks had died in the name of, yet I wasn't doing anything to help those who hadn't benefited as I had. If anything, I was a buffer—the acceptable Black whose ability to assimilate into the white space proves the system is working just fine.

My anger boiled with each book I plowed through. How could FDR—the president who stewarded the nation through a war to save Europe and brought America Social Security and the forty-hour workweek—overlook Black genocide in the American South and exclude Black labor from the New Deal's protections? What could drive the US Public Health Service to inject Black men with syphilis? Why was the FBI tapping Martin's phones and harassing Coretta? Why did the same FBI infiltrate and disrupt the Black Panther Party? How could police assassinate Fred Hampton and just get away with it? Why was our government supporting the destabilization of African nations? How could our own taxpayer-funded CIA flood South Central with cheap cocaine in the 1980s?

The contradictions between our espoused beliefs and our actual practices overwhelmed me. Wherever I looked, I saw the same story: Black people being savagely mistreated by my own government only to face blame and criticism for their mistreatment. Yet, remarkably, whenever I mentioned the word *conspiracy* my white friends waved me off. Not possible, they said. Not our government. We wouldn't do that. But we did. Over and over again.

Meanwhile, as I neared graduation, the conservative backlash against the gains of the civil rights movement kept winning new ground. To keep his job, Bill Clinton poured money into prisons and policing while eviscerating welfare benefits to impoverished families. In California, Ward Connerly successfully orchestrated a ban on affirmative action that would ripple across the country over the next decade. Instrumental to both enterprises were the ideas and attitudes that Bloom, Murray, Dinesh D'Souza, and a coterie of Bradley-funded conservative think-tank experts proliferated. In an endless stream of articles and books blaming poor Black folks for being poor, conservatives made a color-blind case for expanding law enforcement authority to clamp down on crime and against helping those it considered shiftless and ultimately irredeemable.

Though few said it publicly, the conservative narrative was nothing more than a revival of the narratives racists used to justified slavery, the violent rollback of Reconstruction, and the imposition of Jim Crow. The only meaningful difference was the language conservatives used to win our generation's tacit consent. Conservatives knew they would never win us over with the blatant bigotry of their predecessors. So they concealed their racial animus under American values and ideals such as fairness and merit— ideals we had been raised to believe in. They founded deceptively named organizations such as the Center for Individual Rights and the American Civil Rights Institute to undermine actual civil rights laws and reframe policies to protect white advantage.

My assertion is that by the late 1990s, the conservative agenda had become so deeply ingrained in our generation that its arguments seemed like perfectly normal, rational, and necessary extensions of democracy itself. Of course more prisons would protect law-abiding citizens. Certainly cutting welfare would stimulate a strong work ethic. Without question ending racial preferences would restore equal rights for all citizens. These were artfully framed as "commonsense" solutions that any smart, fair-minded American ought to support now that racism had ended. And if a law or policy happened to disproportionately impact Black people, well, at some point Black people just needed to move on from slavery and stand on our own like everyone else.

As I studied and observed, I came to believe that our— mine and yours—disconnection from Black suffering is by design. Neither you nor I identified with or joined ourselves to Black folks at the margins of society because we were fed cherry-picked narratives that confirmed the worthlessness of Black life. The euphemistic "culture of poverty," not systemic oppression, was to blame for the conditions in which so many Black people lived. Black people made bad choices, therefore they did not deserve *our* support. This miseducation has proven purposeful, durable, and infinitely useful. Any immigrant arriving in America and hoping to make it learns early on that Black people occupy the bottom rung. We serve a vital clarifying role, imbuing white America and those striving to access white advantage with a sense of certainty and order. To be white is to be free of terror. Free not to live within its midst. Free to justifiably ignore it. Free to pass judgment and continue on with one's day, untroubled.

Friend, I'm going to ask a hard question and trust you to answer for yourself. Does any of what I just shared resonate with you? Have you ever found yourself witnessing Black suffering and turned the other way? Wished we would stop complaining or protesting or just "making everything racial"? Wished we would shut up and dribble? Just stand for the *damn* flag? In short, have you ever felt as though the public display of Black pain and protest had nothing to do with your American life or your American freedoms?

If the answer is yes, you are not alone. It is both unlikely that you grasp the unrelenting assault on Black life or appreciate the unrequited allegiance Black people have to this country. No, we have not been captains of industry, and relatively few of us have been prominent legislators by comparison. "Yes, only one Black man has held the title of president of the United States, one Black woman has held the title of vice president, and the current Black Supreme Court justice is virtually an apparition." But—and this is no exaggeration—many of the rights we cherish most trace directly back to the liberatory efforts of Black people. In his definitive history of the Reconstruction era, Eric Foner estimates that 180,000 Blacks, fully one-fifth of the Black male population under the age of forty-five, joined the Union's fight in the Civil War. They walked off plantations to fight for a country that had only given them the lash. These hundreds of thousands battled, built fortifications, guarded supply lines, and guided Union soldiers behind Confederate lines. Simply put, the Union does not win the Civil War without formerly enslaved Black people.

Just try to imagine our lives without the Civil War. No

emancipation. No voting rights, however poorly enforced for the next hundred years. No Civil Right Act of 1866, however imperfectly applied even to this day. No Fourteenth Amendment with its Citizenship, Privileges and Immunities, Due Process, and Equal Protection Clauses. None of those ambitious laws—laws that are the bedrock of American jurisprudence—exist without the Civil War, and that war is not won without Black people.

———

Friend,

I would like to tell you that my rage drove me to George Washington University Law School. That I hoped to learn the system so I could change the system. That just wouldn't be true. I landed in law school because I was disillusioned, with everything. Law school lent me the veneer of respectability when in reality I was just renting time. The idea of a grinding nine-to-five job for the next forty years terrified me. The thought of breaking my back for the same system that oppressed me felt intolerable.

Early on, I discovered I wasn't alone. Law school, I found, was bursting with bright young people from every corner of the country (and beyond) who had done well in college and scored high on standardized tests, the ultimate measures of our meritocracy. Law school was a final spit-shine station for middle- and upper-class youth who had followed the rules and thus reaped the rewards of a system that had favored us from the beginning.

I learned the law school game in the first weeks of classes. Law school values students who are quick, alert, and exact. If you correctly answered a professor's obscure procedural question at the drop of a dime, you were considered brilliant. If you deftly spotted an issue and repeated the requisite holding and rationale back word for word on a test, you got an A. The writers who were able to carefully build an argument based on precedent made law review. Philosophical thinking was cute but viewed with suspicion. Challenging the *application* of law fell within the acceptable bounds, but questioning the foundation upon which a law rested was out of the question. Therefore we didn't talk about who could and could not enter a contract, who could and could not serve on a jury, who could and could not own property. What I learned instead was how to protect the property of the rich. Indeed, I was in tax law the same year the Enron scandal was in the news. The same accounting practices Andersen used to hide Enron's losses were taught to us in class. Similarly, I learned in bankruptcy class how to help corporations sidestep their obligations to their creditors. It was never presented that way, but it was clear from the salaries top law firms paid their first-year associates what we were being taught to do and for whom.

More pointedly, we were trained to revere judges who could fashion clever, convoluted, and often counterintuitive opinions rather than those who spoke directly to the principles of justice and injustice, right and wrong. In that first year of law school I discovered the sacred bond between Justices William Brennan and Thurgood Marshall. One white, one Black, they always had each other's back on the most critical social issue, the death penalty. Both stood categorically against it on moral and constitutional grounds, but also because it targeted the same Black people who had faced lynching; yet in our classes we paid only cursory attention to their dissents and never once mentioned the underlying call to conscience—that state-sanctioned killing is abhorrent, which they collectively reiterated in more than twenty-one hundred cases.[36]

I traveled to South Africa to study human rights law the summer after my first year. Little did I know that trip would cement my disaffection for the law and send me on a twenty-year career quest.

By way of context, I landed in Cape Town the day Thabo Mbeki—Nelson Mandela's successor as president—was inaugurated and thrust headlong into a country in the midst of a great transformation. "Apartheid had only officially ended a mere five years earlier, and a new constitution sat squarely at the center of the society being built." In my classes at the University of the Western Cape I learned that the postapartheid government had issued a public call for *anyone* to submit recommendations for the constitution. It received nearly two million responses. The opening line of the resulting law, which passed in 1996, reads, "We, the people of South Africa, Recognise the injustices of our past." And while our constitution—the oldest in the world—prioritizes governmental structure, South Africa's starts with thirty-two articles focused on human rights, including the rights to "dignity," to "fair labour practices," to "form and join a trade union," to "an environment that is not harmful to . . . health or well-being," to "sufficient food and water," and to "access to adequate housing."

To be sure, the country that I encountered was still far from achieving these lofty aspirations. Yet, those aspirations were alive all around me.

On my first weekend trip to a local market, a young man approached me and introduced himself. He offered to help me negotiate my purchases. I had been warned by trip organizers to watch out for friendly interlopers, but I considered myself capable of sizing up a situation and making my own decisions. The young man struck me as trustworthy, so I took him up on his offer and we spent the afternoon together. His name was Pieter and he worked part-time at a clothing store and lived with his girlfriend.

When I was finished shopping, I asked Pieter how much I owed him.

He waved me off. "I didn't help you for that."

Bullshit, I thought, and insisted he let me give him something.

"What about that?" Pieter pointed to the Nike shirt I was wearing.

"I need to wash it first."

We agreed to the exchange, and on the appointed date and time, Pieter buzzed my flat. I told him that I'd meet him in the lobby.

He asked to come up. "I have something for you."

My danger signals shot up. So this was his plan. That whole "I don't want money" thing was part of his scheme to gain my trust, get into my flat, and rob me blind. Well, he obviously didn't know whom he was dealing with.

I met him at the elevator, ready. Then the doors opened.

Pieter was holding a pair of dinner plates. "We figured you could use a proper meal."

In that moment of quiet shame I noticed and named the root of my anxiety. Africans were schemers. They were not to be trusted. I didn't like it and didn't know exactly where I had picked up those stereotypes, but they were inside me and they only required the slightest provocation to rear up.

I soon discovered that damaging stereotypes lived on both sides of the Atlantic when over dinner Pieter asked me if it was okay to call me a "nigger." I almost coughed up my curry, but once I got past the shock of his directness, I could see that Pieter meant the question in earnest. He knew as little about who I really was as I of him. What fragments of information he had acquired about Black America had arrived by way of music videos and Hollywood movies.

To the best of my ability, I explained the history of the word, including the harm it had wrought and the ways some of my peers sought to reclaim its power for our purposes. In the course of things, we each became aware of the lies we had been fed about each other. Through our shared truth seeking and telling, trust started to form.

Later that summer Pieter brought me and a few other

American law students to a club. We each breezed in uneventfully, but the bouncer held Pieter up.

"We're together," I said. The bouncer didn't budge. "What's going on here?"

Pieter looked at me and rubbed his bare forearm. The gesture was all I needed. We left together.

"I don't get it," I said, holding my arm next to his as we headed back to his car. "You and I are the same complexion."

Pieter opened his door and grinned. "You have something I don't."

"What's that?"

"A US passport."

Until that night, I had never thought of myself as an American. But in his country, my citizenship status opened doors that he couldn't walk through. In my brief time in the country in which he had been born, I had toured Parliament and met privately with Supreme Court justices. My summer classmates spent their weekends golfing. Others flew off on safaris. Our American currency gave us the power to live comfortably. I had an ocean-view apartment. My classmates and I enjoyed lavish dinners nightly. We were scooping up art at cut-rate prices and sending it back home. We were driven around on a charter bus and hired taxis whenever it suited us.

At twenty-four, I was experiencing privilege without accomplishment. Just being an American accrued me the rights and protections of empire. It was a strange, disorienting reality to sit with, but I had to own it. In the United States, race took precedence. My rage and much of my identity was fueled by four centuries of injustice. In South Africa, an equally abhorrent injustice had been enacted against people who looked like me. Yet my nationality exempted me.

I would not go as far as to make a direct comparison between my brief brush with privilege in South Africa and white advantage in America, but it nonetheless opened my eyes. In my experience, many white Americans are uncomfortable being identified with or categorized as white. They push back, choosing to identify with their European ancestors or simply as an individual for reasons that I will not try to decipher but are worth exploring on your own. The point is, being placed into a group that they haven't chosen for themselves wounds some white people. It strips them of their right to define who they are. In South Africa, I felt that defensiveness. I was a young Black man. That was my identity. Yet, suddenly, my American nationality was what counted in the eyes of others and thus dictated how I was treated.

The awakening was humbling and hard. I felt like a hypocrite. At home, I railed against American capitalism and charged my white friends with failing to see Black struggles. Abroad, I enjoyed the benefits of being an American and conveniently overlooked the price being exacted so that I could move around freely. Pieter and his girl lived on the outskirts of the city, far away from the upscale coastal region I called home. The depressed wages they were paid—a direct outcome of the extractive underdevelopment wrought by colonialism—attracted American tourists such as me who could live like postcolonial princes and princesses.

Pieter let me process my guilt. Then he consoled me. I wasn't to blame. The entire world had been told that the election of Nelson Mandela had liberated the country from its past, that his presidency wiped away the stains of apartheid.

"It's a great story," said Pieter. "It's just not that simple."

Even after the ratification of the new constitution, Afrikaners maintained their property and wealth, which in turn gave them a disproportionate share of power. They still created the narratives that the world consumed. In Pieter's view, Black faces had been placed in visible authority roles to placate the international community and pacify the populace. Pieter considered Nelson Mandela one of those faces. Pieter wasn't alone. As respected as Mandela was, Winnie Mandela was the people's hero. She had kept his name alive for the twenty-seven years he sat on Robben Island.

Pieter had an idea. "Write about us. Tell our story. Let them know we are here, doing our thing."

The world still knew little about the South African experience and even less about its youth culture.

After that night, Pieter began taking me to underground hip-hop clubs, introducing me to rappers, graffiti artists, dancers, and photographers. I learned that Tupac was their prophet. His image blazed the side of abandoned buildings, T-shirts, and posters. His music pulsed from tinny barbershop booths. In Tupac, they heard their own anguish and anger. In them, I encountered a purity and clarity that I had only known in the brief era of conscious rap that Public Enemy embodied.

Reporting gave me the purpose that I couldn't find in the law. I wasn't concerned with where the story that emerged ultimately landed. My only mission was humanizing a group of young artists living on the margins by contextualizing their experience within a complex history of race, class, and culture.

Each day after classes ended, I dashed to an interview that usually ran long into the night, at which point we headed to a show that, in turn, wandered into the morning. I'd make it back to my flat in time for what felt like a nap before rising to repeat. As I listened to their take on the music I had been raised on, slowly catching on to their slang and dialect, I discovered the same angst and urgency that defined underground hip-hop culture in America. Artists spit lyrics about being harassed by the cops and feeling locked out of opportunity, the struggle to survive in a system that didn't regard their lives or the lives of those they loved as important. They lamented lost friends and prayed for brighter futures. They worried about their sisters, mothers, and little brothers. They feared for their lives. With only modest variations, my South African peers were facing the same physical and psychological terror as my people in America. They had been colonized, enslaved, and shunted into a separate, subjugated society. The apartheid system sought to constrict Black life in every way imaginable. Over time their version of white supremacy had calcified into a self-perpetuating caste system that they were now trying to break.

Witnessing a slightly different version of the same rigged system up close and with the privilege of a US passport that allowed me to move through it all relatively untouched was like peeking behind the veil. In America, every racial event felt personal. Being an American reporter in South Africa gave me the space I needed to observe. And what I saw was that inasmuch as Black Africans treated me as a distant relative, the white Afrikaner did not understand me at all. He mistook me for just another American. The first time this happened was at a local laundromat.

Hearing my American accent, the proprietor, a paunchy middle-aged man, asked if he could have a word. "What do you think of our country?"

"I find it fascinating."

"The crime is out of control," he barked. "We must get tougher. Aren't you afraid?"

"I haven't been threatened by anyone, if that's what you are asking."

Sensing my reticence, the man assured me that he was all for the postapartheid changes. He even pointed to the Black women working for him. "This isn't about that. This is about safety. People are living in fear."

In bars and taxis, white South African men induced me into a similar dialogue again and again, and I found it refreshing and alarming. In America, white men shrouded their prejudices behind the same rationalizations, but the difference was me. I was able to listen to white South Africans without losing my cool. I could probe their thinking without taking it personally. What I learned was that, from their perspective, the anxiety was genuine and rational. But it was also incredibly naive and narrow. Which is to say, these men seemed to lack any sensitivity whatsoever to the root causes of the crimes of which they complained. They seemed to think of crime and the violence that it was often coupled with as arbitrary, apolitical, and ahistorical. They never once paused to consider why people, presumably young, poor, and Black, committed crime, let alone that in their minds they may have been justified.

I could only conclude that the men I spoke to were so desensitized to the injustice surrounding them that they couldn't actually see it. Yes, these men were aware that apartheid had wronged Blacks, but they didn't connect that wrong to their wealth and status. It was as if they were totally independent phenomena. What was more, they honestly felt entitled to judge the conduct of people who the entire world knew had been unjustly oppressed and to call in the authorities at their discretion.

Looking back, I am grateful that these men were too guileless to know better than to reveal their innermost feelings in casual conversation to a Black American. Their naivete granted me a window into how mass delusion works. The deluded genuinely don't regard their ancestors as likely criminals, or, at minimum, collaborators. They believe a system that favors and protects their thievery can still be legitimate. The deluded have limited understandings of the brutality that has been carried out for their comfort. They minimize the grace and humanity of the oppressed. In the case of the white Afrikaners, they should have been grateful for Mandela. Ultimately, he had protected them from slaughter. Yet I'm sure had I said as much, they wouldn't have grasped my gravity.

That fall, I resumed law school, but my real passion was the story. When it was ready, I got in my car and drove to New York. Once there, I looked up the headquarters of every music publication I could find and dropped off copies of a makeshift press packet I had printed and packaged at Kinko's. Only one, a now-defunct radical-left publication called *Blu Magazine*, showed any interest. When my story was published, I mailed copies to Pieter, along with a letter of gratitude for all he had done to make it happen. However, his real and lasting gift was gently helping me notice a major gap in my understanding. It had never even occurred to me that I could be as oblivious of my surroundings as the American white people I was accustomed to criticizing. But rather than cancel me, Pieter put me on a path. That path led to voices and worldviews I would never otherwise have encountered, in large part because I was immersed in a sea of privilege. Indeed, what makes privilege so dangerous in the first place is that it is as invisible as it is insidious.

II

HEAL

The Culture of Charity

The Culture of Expropriation

The Culture of Disbelief

THE CULTURE OF CHARITY

Friend,

In the weeks right after George Floyd's murder on May 25, 2020, and the protests that it sparked, my consulting practice blew up. There's just no other way to put it. When COVID had descended in March 2020, business dried up overnight. No one had money for racial equity. When the Black Lives Matter protests put racism back at the forefront of the conversation, I couldn't keep up with the demand. This personal and professional prosperity as a result of racial injustice was disorienting and at times infuriating. All that I could do was accept that the work needed to be done, use my skills and expertise responsibly, and remain grounded in and cognizant of the rotten root of my abundance.

As the engagements piled up, I was struck by how many of my new clients were dealing with the same internal issue. The younger staff, millennials for the most part, were calling out the older and typically more experienced staff—some Gen Xers but mostly boomers—for enacting racial oppression within their organizations. They were naming practices and policies, norms and values, that in their view perpetuated white-supremacy culture. They were releasing pent-up pain and anger, and they were past the point of conversation and compromise. Now they had demands. Facing an insurrection, fearful, frustrated leaders were turning to the same DEI (Diversity, Equity, and Inclusion) consultants that they had had no money for just a few months earlier. Suddenly, they needed help. Suddenly, the money had appeared.

This pattern was especially true with my nonprofit-sector clients.

I didn't hold these leaders in contempt, but I did make it my business to understand their intentions. Were they trying to check a box or were they serious? I'd had my share of those check-a-box experiences. The most memorable was the time I was hired by a national mentoring organization to run a staff training, only to discover upon arriving that all of the senior leaders were in other meetings and couldn't make it. The staff unleashed its fury on me. They were overworked and underpaid. They didn't have the resources they needed to do their jobs. Their leaders only seemed interested in impressing donors and the board with unrealistic growth plans. When I walked out the door two hours later, beaten up and dispirited, it dawned on me why I had been hired. The leaders needed someone to take their blows for them. I was their paid punching bag.

This go-round, I politely told the leaders who were reaching out for help to please look elsewhere if they just wanted me to give them cover long enough for the protests to die down. After some honest probing, I found that in the vast majority of cases the leaders at least believed their intentions were earnest. They were listening to their staffs. They didn't want to be barriers. They wanted to be part of the solution.

When I asked these leaders what they thought their core issue was, the answer was also staggeringly uniform: Although they worked in BIPIC (Black, Indigenous, and People of Color) communities, served BIPOC people, or in some other way existed to address systemic racism rooted in anti-Blackness, they had few, if any, BIPOC people in senior leadership roles either on staff or on the board.

Even in organizations with higher numbers of BIPOC employees, those staff were frequently relegated to the lower-paid positions with the least access to power, while white staff held the disproportionate share of the higher-paying, decision-making roles. Now the staff, and in some cases even the board, were calling for change.

Remarkably, and despite a trove of national employment statistics showing a consistently stagnant racial-employment gap for decades, the leaders invariably thought their situation was unique. That somehow they alone had failed to hire and promote Black people. It wasn't, I told them. Nonprofits, like individuals, want to believe they are immune to the disease plaguing the larger society. They want to believe that because they are doing good, well-intentioned work and aren't being intentionally racist, that should be enough. Leaders, I found, were thus surprised to learn that their people knew differently all along.

It was never lost on me in these conversations that I might have been the leader on the other end of the line looking for answers had this incarnation of Black Lives Matter occurred just a few years earlier. In 2016, I was leading a nonprofit when police killed Philando Castile and Alton Sterling and BLM protesters took to the streets across the country. Even as I watched it all unfold, it didn't cross my mind to say anything until a young staff member wrote an email to her supervisor, who then forwarded it up the chain to me. In it, she said the youth in her program were angry and afraid. She asked how the organization planned to support her so she could support them. I passed the email up another notch. For the next day, emails flew around. What emerged was a milquetoast, tone-deaf "solidarity" statement that read like classic corporate-speak. Before any blowback could reach my in-box, an army veteran shot and killed five Dallas police officers at a Black Lives Matter march. A week later a former marine shot six Baton Rouge police officers, killing three. Public sentiment swiftly turned against BLM. The media was complicit. Candidate Donald Trump seized the opportunity to drape himself in "all lives matter" rhetoric and promised to clamp down on social unrest. Eventually, what might have been a budding movement for change died down. Within a couple of weeks we all went back to business as usual.

In 2016, I dodged the moment of reckoning that leaders faced in summer 2020. So I empathized with them. Yet, we still need to talk about why so many organizations whose mission is to serve BIPOC communities are led by white people.

Let me preface what I am about to share by stating that in a perfect world it shouldn't matter who is at the helm, especially when it comes to addressing society's biggest challenges such as education and poverty. I agree that the best *person* should have the job regardless of race or gender. But in a perfect world we also wouldn't need nonprofits to solve our biggest problems. In a perfect world we might not need them at all. I don't have to tell you that we don't live in a perfect world. We live in an incredibly unjust and inequitable society, the very legitimacy of which rests on an egalitarian ideal embedded in our founding documents. That ideal serves overlapping but distinct purposes for those at the bottom and those at the top. Charities are the lifeblood of that ideal. By giving comfort to the poor and cover for the rich, they keep an underlying arrangement rooted in white supremacy firmly intact. Collectively, I call this the culture of charity, and most of us buy into its benefits without understanding its harms.

To most Americans, the charity sector operates behind a veil. If anything, it is viewed uncritically as a site of social good. When, for example, I told people I worked at a nonprofit, their eyebrows invariably crested compassionately. Just saying that I worked for a cause that served youth of color endowed me with a near-saintly quality. The charity imprimatur was like a secular seal of approval. I had to be a good person; why else would I choose to help poor people and not make any money?

The veil assuages many well-meaning, well-heeled

white people. They write checks, show up to galas, and join boards without ever reflecting on how much of it is orchestrated to gently tug at their purse strings or why we depend on the charity sector to do things for Black people that the government once did for white people. I liken it to the organic-food industry. The average person can't define the federal requirement for organically raised chickens.[1] What we know is that we are disturbed by the idea of our farm animals being mistreated or injected with chemicals. We don't want to contribute to the cycle of planetary degradation and toxicity, so we buy products labeled organic or locally sourced. We are glad to pay the premium. Not only do we get the health benefits, we get the virtue-signaling benefits of being associated with the eco-friendly lifestyle.

Those of us who work within and around charities quickly discover the sector is far more complex, complicated, and complicit in the perpetuation of racist stereotypes. I found this out early on in my nonprofit career. Shortly after finishing law school and publishing my first book, to make ends meet I took a job working at a nonprofit based near Wall Street that provided job training for high schoolers. Every week I took a train into the office to run life-skills workshops for the teens. The founder was a smart, charismatic guy whose corner office overlooking the East River was about the size of his entire team's row of cubicles. The kids seemed to like him—they all called him by his first name and sometimes played basketball with him.

It didn't take long for the teens to start gravitating toward me. It was to be expected: I was a young Black man with dreads and had multiple degrees yet still identified with the culture. In me, they could see an older version of themselves or just an adult with whom they could relate. I began to mentor a couple of older boys outside work hours. Mostly we played basketball and talked about life and family.

One afternoon as I was entering the office to set up for my workshop, the organization's second-in-command, a Black woman, called me aside for a word. The founder had updated the dress code policies, she said. Moving forward, I had to dress more "professionally" in the office. It didn't take much for me to realize what was happening. My being a lawyer and published author was great. Everyone *loved* that about me. However, my Friday-afternoon attire—hoodies, jeans, and sneakers—all of that likely compounded by my long, locked hair, sent the wrong message. After leaving her office, I peeked into the big boss's office. I hoped to have a word. The office was empty.

Initially, I assumed that the leader had changed the policy because I wasn't performing the image of professionalism that he had decided was best for these Black children to see and emulate. I was offended and hurt. In my view, I was showing them exactly the opposite; that, just like techies who wore T-shirts to work, they didn't have to conform to mainstream standards to be successful. When Wall Street collapsed a few months later and the organization was on the brink of bankruptcy, I found out who and what was really behind the move. Amid the layoffs and austerities it came to light that the board chair and main benefactor was a big deal at Lehman Brothers.

All along I had thought I was working for a charity *on* Wall Street when in reality I was working *for* a Wall Street bank. That was my initial introduction to the dirty little secret that drives social-justice work in America. For activists, idealists, outcasts, nonconformists, dissidents, exiles, and creatives, the 501(c)(3) seal tends to mean shelter, safe harbor, and salvation—it is Batman's Bat-Signal in the seedy Gotham sky. We arrive with high ideals, lived experiences within communities of color, and expertise paid for by hefty student loans, only to find out that, when it comes down to it, we still work for a bank. The same people who, to give just one example, pumped Black communities with the predatory loans that helped trigger the financial crisis were also directing social-change efforts in those communities. In short, the ideologies and prerogatives of wealth rule the charity sector. By and large, wealthy white men set the standards of success and decide which charities are worth investing in. They choose who leads these charitable endeavors. Unsurprisingly, the leaders they choose carry credentials that wealthy white people value most: degrees from elite schools, brief stints at a top consulting firm and/or investment bank, perhaps preceded by a stop at Teach For America. These leaders serve at the pleasure of wealthy white benefactors, not the community or even the staff.

————

As I wove through the New York City and Southern California nonprofit scenes over the next decade, rising from junior to more senior roles, I gained access to boards, and deeper insight into the relationship between social justice and the society pages. Invariably, the organizational staff whitened the closer I got to the top. Inevitably, powerful white men along with a sprinkling of white women and even a person of color here and there occupied the seats in the boardroom. When I became a nonprofit leader myself, I built solid and sometimes intimate working relationships with these people. I found them genuine, likable, and well intended. They didn't put on airs or flaunt their wealth. They genuinely cared about the cause. But they also held unwavering, unexamined ideas about what the underlying problems were, how to solve them, and the checkbooks and networks that gave them the deciding vote.

I learned a lot in those boardrooms. For powerful people, the solution to the absence of positive role models in the community wasn't justice reform; it was a corporate volunteer program. The solution to the achievement gap wasn't funding education equitably for children; it was re- placing public education with school choice. The solution to the "opportunity gap" wasn't environmental justice; it was exposure trips outside the inner city. The solution to unequal college access wasn't free college for all; it was a scholarship program for worthy kids.

The boardroom conversations I participated in never broadened to explore why there were so few role models, so many low-performing school systems, so few outdoors options, and so much need for financial assistance all con- centrated in one community that also happened to be over- whelmingly Black and Brown. The culture of charity carved these deeply connected problems into separate "causes" that the wealthy could choose to champion buffet-style without having to take any ownership for the long-standing and primordial injustice that undergirded the whole damn thing. In short, I learned that charity culture treats the symptoms but not the disease of racism, obscuring the role that policies benefiting the wealthy—tax cuts, tax credits, privatization, and deregulation—play in maintaining racial inequality. And the culture does this even as charities themselves exploit entrenched racialized symbols, stories, and stereotypes to fuel their missions.

Thus, charities present pictures of cheerful white volunteers helping poor Black children. They present flattering impact data without also acknowledging the incredible, exhausting labor that staff, usually of color, put in to produce it. They use safe, color-blind terms such as *underaccessed, underserved, under-resourced,* or *underprivileged*—terms that obscure this country's history of oppression and marginalization. They tell overly simplified turnaround stories that highlight individual effort and downplay systemic obstacles. They even choose and coach the most "well-spoken" participants to meet with donors. Charities do all of this for the benefit of wealthy white audiences whose generosity keeps the lights on.

The annual fundraiser is where it all comes together in what I can only describe as an ensemble celebration of white saviorism. No matter how seemingly diverse or inclusive, these gala events still boil down to the same staid stereotypes. You know exactly what I am talking about. I'm sure you have attended your share of these events. In New York, Cipriani is synonymous with gala season. First, the nonprofit stuffs you with filler foods and plies you with midgrade alcohol. Then it seats you at a cramped table and inundates you with heartwarming stories about the nonprofit's extraordinary impact on the lives of its less fortunate participants. Then the auctioneer steps onstage and things get really creepy. Back in the day, rich people raised paddles to announce their generosity. The room applauded, and nonprofit staff scampered around collecting checks and promissory notes. Nowadays, text-to-bid technology has made things a little more tactful and discreet. The names and donations scroll across the big screen.

You probably have no idea how humiliating these events can feel for those of us involved, especially BIPOC staff who got into this work to change inequitable systems. A nonprofit where I once worked used to gather the entire staff the day of the gala for a pep talk. We were told to make our guests feel special. We were reminded to spread ourselves around and mingle, just not too freely. One year I and the other Black guy in the office were assigned to van duty—we had to drive all of the guest gift bags to the venue and bring everything left behind back to the office once the gala ended. Another year, I was a greeter. A colleague, the Black woman who oversaw programs nationally, and I stood like smiling sentries as New York's moneyed class exited black cars and ascended into yet another night of ego stroking and entertainment. Among them was a Sidwell classmate who either didn't recognize me or spared us both the embarrassment.

Of the many soul-crushing gala stories my BIPOC friends have told me over the years, one in particular illustrates just how toxic these events can be. Shortly after graduating from a liberal arts college in New England and starting at a prominent investment bank, a mentee recalled speaking at a gala for a charity he'd once participated in back in high school. The staff helped him write his speech, advising him to emphasize how the program helped him overcome the challenges of growing up in a single-parent household in an underserved community.

"In the middle of delivering the speech, I looked out and saw my mother," he said. "Then I looked beside her and saw my stepdad."

His heart sank. His stepfather had been in his life since he was a little boy, yet had been scrubbed from the story.

Charity culture warps us all in two fundamental ways: by its omissions and its exaggerations. It appropriates stereotypes of broken communities, homes, and schools that already live in society to fuel a poverty-to-prosperity mythos that aligns neatly with meritocracy. Just as public assistance programs punish deadbeat dads, two working parents in the home doesn't jibe with charity culture. Unable or unwilling to explain how my mentee could have a father in the home and still need financial assistance for college, the charity coached him to omit his stepdad. In doing so, it both exaggerated its role in his uplift and silenced a deeper indictment of the neoliberal policies to which so many in the audience subscribe and upon which so much private wealth has been accumulated.

But here's the kicker: I get it. I *really* do. When I became a leader and had to raise a multimillion-dollar budget each year to pay my staff, I found myself facing uncomfortable choices. I spent a lot of time inside Upper East Side offices and apartments. Over time, I found myself drifting further from my staff and deeper into the orbit of my board members. They became my real constituents, the people whose praise I sought and favor I curried allegedly in the name of the mission, but actually to advance my career. I justified compromises of my values in the name of the cause. On balance, I told myself, we were doing more good than harm. I knew the line, I said, and I wouldn't cross it. But the more I pushed my staff to meet outrageous grant expectations, made promises to board members to serve more people in more places, requested new stories to serve up to funders, and imposed spur-of-the-moment donor visits on the program, the blurrier the line became. Over time, I lost the respect of my staff. I became the corner-office executive director that I had once despised.

I hit my breaking point when a board member called and said that a friend—someone who had been generous to the charity in the past, she reminded me—had a request. The board member put me in touch with the friend, who told me over text that her daughter needed to fulfill her community-service requirements right away and she was eager to volunteer with disadvantaged kids.

"I was thinking she could help them with their homework or help feed them or help the staff run some of the activities."

"How old is your daughter?"

"Twelve."

"Well, the kids in the program are that age."

I let my comment linger, but the woman didn't register what I was getting at.

"Maybe your daughter can join the program as a participant."

The woman abruptly stopped texting. I never heard from her again.

The conversation was a gut punch. Charity culture had so warped this woman's way of seeing and thinking—her mind-set—that she couldn't imagine that kids of color didn't need anything from her daughter other than friendship. Nor could she fathom that they might have something to teach her daughter other than how to be a good white person who gave back to the poor little children of color.

These and other experiences drove me to reflect deeply on my experiences in the nonprofit sector. I had witnessed and in too many instances been quietly complicit in conversations wherein powerful, well-intentioned white people, men especially but not exclusively, based big decisions on a worldview that a charity's ultimate measure of impact and success was the extent to which poor people and people of color assimilated to middle-class white values. No one ever said it so openly, but let's be honest: the charity model wasn't set up to change society. Not only do the laws governing 501(c)(3)s expressly prohibit political activism, tax avoidance and wealth preservation were the foundational function of philanthropy. Spoken or not, the belief underlying the establishment of most nonprofit organizations is that the system is generally just fine; it's people who are broken. And we are here to fix them. Consider the words of Frederick Gates, one of the architects of the Rockefeller Foundation and trustee of the General Education Board. In his 1913 book, *The Country School of To-Morrow,* Gates wrote of the board's intentions toward its rural supplicants:

"We shall not try to make these people or any of their children into philosophers or men of learning or of science. We are not to raise up among them authors, orators, poets, or men of letters. We shall not search for embryo great artists, painters, musicians. Nor will we cherish even the humbler ambition to raise up from among them lawyers, doctors, preachers, statesmen, of whom we now have ample supply."[2]

Today, many charities are being forced by their people— usually younger staff of color and white allies—to challenge this assumption. They are pushing back on the notion that white is right. They want to change the system. They want to put an end to what many call "poverty porn"—the abasing of their culture and erasure of context to cater to white sensibilities and wealth. Only time will tell if white money is willing to pay for the dismantling of white dominance.

I started consulting for organizations in turmoil with my own experiences in mind. I understood the layers and divides in a way that gave me insight into the tensions within. I knew how the average privileged white person who sat on boards and led nonprofits had been educated around race. I was educated right alongside them. That education had left out critical context. It led us to falsely believe that racism was a minor problem that had by and large been solved or that it was just too big and not worth tackling at all. It was important to my own healing that I challenged myself and my clients to be brave with one another, to be in community with one another, to learn our history together, and to be honest and humble in inquiring into one another's stories.

I still believe charities can play an important role in our society. They just have to adapt to a paradigm in which people of color who are doing the work are demanding the right to define the problems and shape the solutions facing their communities. As allies, white people—especially white men—are being asked to give up the reins even as they are still being called upon to commit resources. I can imagine this presents a contradiction that needs to be reconciled. To the victor go the spoils is the axiom American capitalism holds most sacred. Wealth and power are self-justifying and self-reinforcing. Those who have accumulated both are bestowed with the unassailable right to rule.

To move forward, we have to try a different mental model guided by fellowship and rooted in trust. To get started, accept that the people closest to the good work know better than you. Speak with them. Listen to them. Learn from them. Follow their lead. They are the experts. When they tell you what is needed, give it freely. If you have it, let it go. Do not meet about it at the next quarterly meeting. Don't make them wait for you to get around to it. Don't make them beseech you at the altar of your largesse. Don't make them jump through every hoop to gain your trust and prove their merit, especially when the standards are themselves based on unfair access.

Understand that an injustice has been done, a deep unresolved harm that spans time and has seeped into every orifice of society. That harm has advantaged white people and disadvantaged everyone who is not or could not become white. Over time, that injustice allowed white people to accumulate so much land, wealth, and power that it is impossible to balance the scales without a massive, sustained wealth transfer. And while you were not personally involved in the formation of this behemoth, you were born into it. You were raised in it. And by virtue of a socially constructed race lottery, it opened doors and allowed you to bypass barriers and roadblocks. In that light, giving is not charity to the less fortunate. It is reparations to the wronged. It is healing in and of itself. It is its own reward. So just embrace that and release the need to control outcome, determine impact, or otherwise turn our liberation into your latest change initiative.

THE CULTURE OF EXPROPRIATION

Friend,

I was working just blocks from Zuccotti Park in the Financial District when *Adbusters* magazine issued the first call for America's disaffected to Occupy Wall Street. The first ragtag protest happened right outside the windows of my office building. Over the days that followed, the daily protests puttered along almost comically. The Tahrir Square uprising notwithstanding, few expected those initial daily marches through the Financial District to spark a sustained movement, certainly not one that rippled across the country.

Then the State of Georgia refused to grant clemency to a Black death row inmate and convicted murderer named Troy Davis. The Davis case had made headlines and garnered support from President Jimmy Carter to Archbishop Desmond Tutu. Witnesses had recanted. Evidence had been called into question. And then there was the ever-present factor of race. Mark Allen MacPhail, the victim, was white. In Georgia, prosecutors and juries had been shown to condemn Blacks for killing whites at a significantly higher rate than the other way around. Once again, the upshot was that white life was worth more.

The state's ruling meant that Davis was going to die the next day. In response, his supporters put out a call for an emergency demonstration at Zuccotti Park (aka Liberty Plaza). After giving a radio interview about Davis's death sentence, I walked over to the park to stand vigil at an emergency demonstration. As I stood among a multiracial, multigenerational crowd listening to an outpouring of pain, I distinctly felt the real occupation begin in earnest. Over the weeks and months that followed, few reports made the connection between Davis and Occupy. Having witnessed the early days and the shift that occurred, I can say that his death centered and grounded a gathering into a movement.

After that day, I made a point of walking through the camp daily, stopping to observe the General Assembly or talk with residents. I didn't consider myself an active participant in the movement then and won't attempt to puff up my activist credentials now, but I was engaged all the same. Occupy's indignation over wealth inequality was fueling a long-overdue national dialogue about economic justice. Its amorphous scope aligned young people seeking relief from crushing student debt to death-penalty abolitionists. Its flat structure bucked convention. Its elusiveness frustrated critics. And for me at least, the movement's forced eviction from visible and valuable spaces across the country echoed the inner-city to urban face-lift I'd witnessed over two decades in three different metropolises.

I'd watched D.C. go condo crazy in the late 1990s and early 2000s, Brooklyn become a hipster haven post-9/11, and Jersey City refashion itself as the sixth borough in the prerecession aughts. In each case, the intrepid white bohemians arrived first. They settled in and set up a sprinkling of relatively innocuous coffee shops and divey bars, but otherwise blended into the existing tapestry. Yet, their mere presence alone signaled opportunity. The local real estate market took notice. What was once considered an unsafe or otherwise undesirable ghetto became an "up-and-coming" enclave pulsing "culture." A fresh new name that none of the current residents had been consulted about emerged. Rental and home prices quietly climbed. Construction began in long-vacant lots and properties left in disrepair for decades. Soon, moving trucks bearing the bohemians' more affluent, less hip professional peers— academics, tech and nonprofit professionals—arrived. A wave of new businesses popped up on the main thorough-fare. By the time Starbucks arrived, the neighborhood had turned.

It wouldn't have occurred to me to wonder about my role in all that was happening back in the fall of 2011 had I not just moved into my latest New York neighborhood at the same time New York City billionaire mayor Michael Bloomberg was evicting the last Occupiers from Zuccotti Park. A lesser-known Harlem neighborhood bounded by 135 and 155 to the south and north and Edgecombe Avenue and Riverside Drive to the east and west, Hamilton Heights had gone through the typical urban phases of ethnic occupancy, flight, and blight. Named after the nation's first treasury secretary, Alexander Hamilton, farms initially occupied the area. After the Revolutionary War, large country estates appeared, followed by elegantly designed row houses in the nineteenth century. By the early twentieth century, sprawling apartments, most of which remain sturdy reminders of our nation's craftsmanship and quality, had been erected. At that time, the residents were middle-class professionals of Irish, Italian, and German stock. Middle-class Black professionals began making their way into the section now widely known as Sugar Hill in the twenties and thirties. Ralph Ellison, W. E .B. Du

Bois, Thurgood Marshall, Paul Robeson, Count Basie, and Langston Hughes would be among the prominent Black folks who would call Hamilton Heights home. As was the case throughout the long, checkered history of integration, Black entrance spurred white exit, and by the middle of the twentieth century the neighborhood was showing the signature symptoms of suburban flight. Beginning in the 1960s and '70s, the Dominican Republic's turbulent political and economic climate drove millions off one island and onto another. By the time I arrived, the blocks surrounding my building were largely Latinx and, based on the goods and services on Broadway, predominantly low income. Though my six-story prewar building had elegance and charm, it wasn't uncommon to spot blunt butts on the stairwell or a discarded Cheetos bag on the landing.

That initial wondering about my role in all of this led me on a Google-supported fact-finding mission into the world of US Census data one night. While I wasn't surprised to discover that New York City had the highest income inequality in the country, I was shocked to find a recent report citing Hamilton Heights as home to the city's widest income gap.[3]

I dug deeper. Over the previous decade, roughly 17 percent of the neighborhood's Black and Latinx populations had departed and been replaced by higher-earning, higher-ed-degree-holding whites. Not at all surprisingly, rent and property values had soared.

I dug even deeper. The summer before I moved in, the real estate section of *The New York Times* had run an upbeat feature on Hamilton Heights.[4] The main body of the story read like a glorified ad for a new satellite campus that nearby Columbia University was building on seventeen acres of land that the story blithely referred to as "a motley collection of warehouses and garages" in an area "largely unknown to those who have never cracked the 100s on the No. 1 train." Buried at the bottom, almost as an afterthought, the story turned, almost obligatorily, to the nagging detractors of progress: "Of course, one person's cool new cafe is another's sign that the neighborhood is about to be ruined by gentrification. And there is no shortage of people in Hamilton Heights who fear Columbia's arrival."

I hadn't known about, let alone factored in, Columbia's expansion into my move. I definitely didn't see myself as a gentrifier. I drove a twenty-year-old car that my mother had given me when she upgraded. I worked at a nonprofit. I had a mountain of student debt. I was Black. Yet, based on the data, my household income put me a lot closer to the top than the bottom fifth of the brackets.

That next day I walked out to the Riverside Drive Viaduct, overlooking Columbia's construction zone. From a vacant building buttressing the work site, a banner hung facing the Henry Hudson Parkway. In plaintive, bold letters, it read DEAR COLUMBIA: NO FORCED DISPLACEMENT.

The banner hit me hard. When I was growing up, my dad had purchased a row house near D.C.'s old U Street Corridor for his new engineering firm. He hired a group of young Black engineers and draftsmen. He made an earnest effort to root himself in the neighborhood, and the early years were promising. Then crack barnstormed the block. His office was repeatedly robbed. I remember catching a woman turning a trick and a couple freebasing in the alley behind the building. Eventually, my father sold a building now worth over $1 million for $78,000. Dispirited, exhausted, and frustrated, he moved to California to start fresh.

Almost as soon as my father left, the city started its turnaround. Even after I moved away and he passed on, I always made a point of returning to the building whenever I was back. I'd drive by and pull over, just to look at it and remember. The building stood as a marker of time, a reminder of what could have been and a symbol of the shadows in which so much of Black America's experience resides. As crack receded and white people appeared, the area became visible and viable. But I could never forget my dad's struggle and its ultimate futility. It bothered me that his attempt to invest in and build up the community hadn't catalyzed capital investment or corralled law enforcement in the way the arrival of white people had. It was as if he—and by extension so many others—hadn't even existed. Their stories didn't count. There was blight and then there was white.

I landed an assignment to write that story in the fall of 2011. In the several weeks I spent reporting, I learned more about the people and policies that had shaped D.C. than in all my years of education combined. Just before I packed up and returned to New York to begin writing, I invited two dozen residents ranging in age, identity, and occupation to participate in a conversation about race and class in the city. The question I placed before them was what, in their view, was the problem. An older Black woman announced that gentrification was part of "the plan," a popular conspiracy theory that has floated around D.C. for so long that it has its own Wikipedia page. The theory asserts that whites intentionally orchestrated the city's decline and the destruction of the Black community to discredit Black leadership and regain control. Gentrification, she insisted, was the natural result. As preposterously paranoid as the idea of a master plan to retake the city sounded to the group and probably sounds to you, I'm going to ask you to withhold judgment while I list a few historical facts:

- The Indian Removal Act of 1830
- The annexation of 55 percent of Mexico in 1848
- The forced taking of the Philippines
- The forced taking of Puerto Rico
- The forced taking of Hawaii
- Japanese internment camps
- The destruction of a thriving Black community in Tulsa, Oklahoma
- The destruction of a thriving Black community in Rosewood, Florida
- Past and present-day redlining
- The abandonment of Black New Orleanians during and after Hurricane Katrina
- Predatory lending leading to the subprime mortgage crisis that wiped out billions in Black wealth

This is just a short list but, I hope, you get where I am going with this. Our American history is simply too rife with documented instances in which land occupied by people of color has forcibly been taken, preyed upon, intentionally devalued, or flat out destroyed for any well-meaning white people to roll their eyes when an old Black woman says that she believes that white people had an organized plan to take land occupied by Black people in D.C. It is a hard truth to face, but it is our truth and we must face it together. White people take the land they desire from people of color. That is a reality. It is not conjecture or conspiracy. Gentrification is part of a tradition of rapacious expansionism and extermination. It is inextricably linked to that legacy of violence and domination. Generations of forcible property seizure has numbed and blinded white people to the deep historical harm that their fellow citizens of color experience whenever yet another space they occupy is taken away. It has made well-intended white people complicit in this tradition of organized theft. Collectively, I call this the culture of expropriation, and it is another way in which racism harms white people.

The effects of this culture are felt most viscerally and violently in the ongoing struggle for physical space, but it lives across society and within all industries. It traces back to the arrival of the first Europeans on Native lands. The culture endures because white supremacy endures.

You may be shaking your head. *Not the same thing,*

you may be thinking. *Totally different.* Buying or renting a property in a blighted Black neighborhood is in no way comparable to forcibly removing Native people from their land. You saw a deal. You made an investment. You joined the block association. You became part of the community. But what you fail to take into consideration is why there was blight in the first place. Moreover, how do we explain the relative abundance of cheap property and land in Black communities? Why is it that Black people are unable to buy low and sell high in white neighborhoods at the same rates? Paying fair market value for a property that is freely available to all and just happens to be much cheaper than a comparable property in a white neighborhood may not be racism per se. It needn't be. Rather, it is the direct *effect* of racism, the result of assorted racist ideas that in turn established a set of social and economic arrangements that have made the housing market favorable to white renters and buyers.

Just as the average white person doesn't have to commit any racist acts to benefit from racism, a white gentrifier similarly doesn't have to move any Black people off their land to benefit from the culture of expropriation. That work has been done, that foundation built and reinforced. The land on which Black people anywhere in the United

States live has already been structurally undervalued by the interaction of evolving policies, practices, norms, and beliefs that assign whiteness advantages and color disadvantages.

Consider the DEAR COLUMBIA banner hanging in Harlem. It wasn't "fear" that local critics were expressing as *The New York Times* suggested. Fear is a fiction that white people pedal to relieve their guilt about the obvious theft. Framing anger as fear is condescension passing as compassion. It suggests that those under the threat of displacement don't have good reason to protest. In fact, it was frustration. It was bitterness. Black folks know exactly what is about to go down when white folks start showing up.

By the same token, I knew that in a year or two, once Columbia's expansion had sparked more commercial interest, I would get a letter from my landlord stating the rent was being jacked up. I would be pushed on to the next colony. That was how I'd ended up in Hamilton Heights. I was a Black middle-class placeholder until someone whiter and wealthier came along.

What about you? Do you know the purpose that you serve in the scheme of things?

———

In reporting my D.C. gentrification story, I met an econ-
omist named Alice Rivlin. In the mid-1990s, Bill Clinton
appointed Rivlin vice-chair of the Federal Reserve. After
that, Congress appointed her to chair the D.C. Financial
Control Board, a body set up by Newt Gingrich upon the
incredible reelection of Mayor Marion Barry to override
his or the city council's fiscal decisions that Republicans
deemed unsound.[5] Essentially, Rivlin served as Chocolate
City's white overseer.

Back in 2001, Rivlin had coauthored a Brookings Institute paper envisioning a fiscally healthy D.C. in ten years.[6]
"African Americans retain a slight majority," she wrote,
"and immigrants from Central America, Asia, and even
Africa are a significant presence." Notably, she didn't mention white people, a fact I have since found at once reveal-
ing and curious. Though the paper didn't recommend a
pathway to solvency, it offered two choices. The first option
was to attract middle-class families with children. The
problem with this option was that it required higher taxes
on everyone to improve schools. Wealthier people wouldn't
tolerate that and would leave or avoid the city, reducing
an already-limited tax base. In fact, D.C.'s financial woes
always had as much to do with its being taxed like a state
yet not having the revenue-raising authority of a state as

with the commonly asserted poor leadership. Option two was attracting young, upper-income singles and couples with cool stuff such as restaurants, shops, and entertainment venues. Rivlin warned that option two would pose a "serious risk of exacerbating racial and class tensions," but it would bring in hundreds of millions in new revenue.

Both options centered on the already-advantaged white and wealthy at the expense of long-standing Black residents. One sought to keep whites from fleeing. The other sought to attract them. When Anthony Williams used his second inaugural speech in 2003 to present his blueprint to build fifteen thousand new homes and bring in one hundred thousand residents within ten years, the die was certainly cast.

At that same D.C. gathering in which the older Black woman protested "the plan," a young white newbie—the archetype Rivlin conjured more than a decade earlier—offered her take on the tense racial situation. She grew up only hearing about official Washington, not D.C. As far as she knew, there was no local history worth knowing. Indeed, the culture of expropriation rests on the premise that nothing of value existed prior to the arrival of white people, and that only upon the civilization of land by whites does history begin.

From where I stand, not in judgment I hope you know by now, you keep choosing to ignore what's in front of you. This pathological unwillingness to connect the past with the present, in this case the capital investment that the mere whiff of whiteness attracts, is characteristic of the culture of expropriation. When you have all the resources and opportunities at your disposal, it is too tempting, too easy, to resist. Simply put, the rewards of being white in this society vastly outweigh the risks of being not-white. You and I both know that. That, too, is by intent. Bacon's Rebellion taught that lesson early in the American experiment. When your ancestors and my ancestors organized in resistance, slaveholders suddenly assigned your people to the white race and consigned mine as chattel. In that way, your ancestors became willing agents in a centuries-long project of elevating, adapting, and perpetuating whiteness. Three centuries later, Rivlin didn't have to force Anthony Williams's hand. She merely had to present the only conceivable choice. Displacement was not the collateral damage or unintended consequence but the known outcome of gentrification. Yet again the interests of Black people (freedom, liberation) were pitted against the interests of white people. Yet again white people's interests prevailed.

The culture of expropriation makes us all instruments

in ensuring that America stays true to President Andrew Johnson's "a country for white men" edict at whatever cost. It poisons the shared well of our humanity. If you are fine with that, then Godspeed. But if you are not fine, you must make different choices. You must choose to relinquish the marker of whiteness by rejecting the privilege of pillaging communities of color for profit and personal gain. You must say, "No, I will not allow myself to be the tool of dominance"—because make no mistake, that is what you are. Just as I am the target of dominance and exploitation.

As Rivlin and Williams knew, as Columbia knew, as Mike Bloomberg knew, gentrification is the contemporary corollary of the expansionist mind-set. Americans are restless people. Each generation requires renewal. New soil to till. Each hopes to seize its birthright for a song, even calling it a "steal." Your parents paved roads and cleared forests to build suburbs. White bankers doled out low- and no-down-payment mortgages to whites only. Our generation in turn repatriated to blighted inner cities, gut-renovating gargantuan brownstones into stylish apartments and making a tidy mint off rentals. In either instance, bodies of color were systemically kept out, priced out, or just shuffled along to accommodate inviolable principles of progress for white people at whatever cost to everyone else. No one can argue that two generations—Xers and Millennials—of educated, affluent white people haven't thrown a lifeline to cities. It just needs to be said with a bit more humility and candor that their white elders also had a hand in the demise of these neighborhoods in the first place.

Writing my D.C. story was a healing exercise. It scratched an infernal itch. As soon as the piece was out in the world, a weight lifted off my chest. I had said everything I needed to say about the first city I had loved, but more important, I had explored the root of white America's compulsion to seize and control. We are all following a script that was written for us long ago. The seizing of African bodies and of Native lands established a cultural blueprint but also a baseline for our future political economy. Our laws, customs, governance, and wealth-distribution system all flows from that reservoir of robbery, which remains the most common crime in this country. Our settler ancestors justified their violence through freedom. One was a necessary and noble means to an ordained end that, ironically, kept finding new frontiers that demanded clearing. In this light, settler colonialism is a "structure, not an event," as historian Patrick Wolfe notes.

In an urban postindustrial context, that original violent settler mentality gets sublimated through saccharine renewal slogans that promise pie-in-the-sky benefits. We—you and I—must be more honest and then turn that honesty into action. We cannot stop the cycle of exploitation until we call it out and commit to corrective actions. Just bringing people together and having an honest conversation is a start. But this is where investing in equity and equality matters most. We are not starting from the same place. White people have more wealth and more access. Thomas Piketty said it best: wealth accumulates value faster than wages rise. At our current pace we will never level the playing field. We need new solutions, and those take time. In the interim, we can start with grace.

A couple of years back a white dog walker caught Black fury when he insisted on using Howard University's grounds as his personal dog park. In response to the criticism he received, the man suggested that "the Yard," a national historic landmark, move.

The first step in unlearning the culture of expropriation is accepting that it is real, still present, and that it often reveals itself as entitlement. The second is challenging and questioning the underlying beliefs that prop up the expropriation mind-set and perpetuate its acceptance. In this case, unless the dog walker is willing to ask himself why he believes his liberty interests supersede those of a long-standing Black community that he has entered, he will never be able to uncover the roots of his affliction. For those who make it that far, the third step is assuming the posture of a guest in someone's home. Guests accept that they don't know the rules. They watch. They ask questions. They learn. And if no one else is letting his or her dog poop on the local HBCU campus, they show some restraint and respect.

Similarly, notice the next time you feel yourself judging a Black community based purely on appearances. Catch yourself. This is the attitude that has justified the use of state power to wrestle away land; and the denial of opportunity to secure better futures. A Black neighborhood may indeed look unsafe or unkempt to you, but that does not mean the community doesn't care, isn't connected to the land, or isn't deserving of better treatment. It means it is experiencing the structural symptoms of poverty. Gentrification treats those symptoms but does not heal the underlying ailment. Only we can do that work. We begin not by asking what is wrong with people and why they are not more like us, but by asking why this came to be in the first place, how have we been complicit up to now, and what is our role in healing.

THE CULTURE OF DISBELIEF

Friend,

Yesterday, a grand jury exonerated Breonna Taylor's killers. A week ago the City of Louisville paid her family a $12 million settlement. I am sitting with the weight of both actions and wondering what such a sum matters to a family who will never be whole again. As is the case every morning, my toddler daughter and I had breakfast. She tossed her cereal and eggs on the floor and I picked it all up. She baited me into a game of chase, and I squatted down and crawled after her giggles. At forty, I couldn't picture bringing a child into this world. At forty-five, fatherhood is my highest calling. This morning, I had to think about losing my baby girl abruptly and unjustly and then being told no wrongdoing occurred. It isn't the first time I've looked at her and felt my heart well up with anguish and my mind go blank with fear, and maybe that's the point.

Have you ever looked at your daughter, worried that

the people our taxes support and upon whom our laws bestow unique authority and immunity will break into her home and shoot her dead? And have you also ever felt utterly powerless to do anything to stop it?

I wish the answer were no, but right now I need the answer to be yes. Feel this moment fully. Breathe it in. What you are experiencing is racism in real time. The case turned on whether the cops announced themselves before forcing their way into her home. Taylor's boyfriend said again and again that the officers did not. He believed they were being burglarized, so he fired the single warning shot that set off more than twenty-five bullets from police. Eleven witnesses also said that they did not hear the cops announce themselves. Yet, in its decision, the grand jury relied on a twelfth witness who also originally said he did not hear the cops announce themselves but later changed his story after a third interview with authorities.

The grand jury chose its allegiance to the culture of white disbelief that perpetuates doubt and denialism in and disregard for the stories Black people tell America about their experiences. That disbelief is killing us.

Over the past few months, the term *systemic racism* has gone viral. I hear and see it all over the place. The naming of the problem has been important. The conservative-backed color-blindness movement of the 1990s made *racism* a curse word and anyone who uttered it paranoid, an opportunist looking to cash in on white guilt or a sad sack reaching for an excuse to explain away his failures. Now, at least, we can say the word *racism* out loud again and not get shouted down or waved off. What wakes me up at night is my fear that in naming the problem we mistakenly believe we have a shared understanding of its depth and complexity. I fear, as always, that we think we are ready to take action when we still have lots of learning ahead.

Racism's secret sauce is and has always been that it hides in plain sight. Its most vulgar expressions—slavery, lynching, land theft, the Klan, Donald Trump—are so obviously vile that most of us can comfortably tell ourselves that we're not racist since we're not or would never do *that.* That disgust with and desire to distance ourselves from racism's ugliest expressions blocks us from probing beneath the surface. We are so repelled by the *effects* of racism, by the ways it shows up in society, that we never develop the lens or language to interrogate the allegedly self-evident, "commonsense" values and beliefs that perpetuate race-based inequality.

Speaking from my own experience, I needed a long time to grasp how racism was different from prejudice or bias. I thought they were all just different words with the same meaning. The idea that racism is prejudice or bias enacted by someone who holds or is backed by the power of a system that advantages whites and disadvantages Blacks struck me as a bit far-fetched and over-the-top. I mean, come on now. People being racist I could get with, but an institution? A system? An entire society? How could inanimate objects be racist anyway? They require people to give them life, and if the people within them aren't prejudiced, then how could an institution or system be? Furthermore, a racist institution, system, or society would depend on lots of people—millions—who have never even met in some instances, let alone agreed to perpetuate discrimination, acting in conscious coordination.

As you can see, I was overthinking it.

Let's get to the brass tacks. The dominant group decides what its society will reward and what it will condemn. The systems within the society adopt and codify those beliefs and values into laws. Institutions within a given system turn those laws into policies and practices. People working within institutions carry out those policies and practices. In that way, we are complicit with the status quo whether we choose to accept that or not.

Ironically, I started to learn how systemic racism works

the weekend before my last year of law school began. I had just returned from a monthlong backpacking tour of Europe with my best friend, Derek, a white guy I'd met on a basketball court in college but bonded with over blunts, bongs, and boxed wine. For me, the trip was a wistful goodbye to youth. I'd taken the Eurorail from Paris to Amsterdam, bunked in a seedy youth hostel in Barcelona, and enjoyed a seventy-two-hour romance in Madrid with a woman from Australia. Once third year began, the party was over. I was ready to focus on graduation and getting a job . . . so you can imagine how disorienting it must have felt to find myself handcuffed in the back seat of a squad car the Friday before school began.

How did I wind up in the back seat of a squad car? Good question. I was standing on a corner with my roommate, also a largish Black male third-year, who had just returned a pair of DVDs to Blockbuster. We were figuring out our dinner plan when he grabbed the construction scaffold above our heads and did a pull-up. Maybe two. By the time he came down, a cop car had parked in front of us. The passenger-side door sprang ajar.

"Down on your knees, hands behind your neck!"

It's worth noting that I had just studied criminal procedure and constitutional law the previous semester. I asked what law I had broken. The cop didn't answer. Instead, she called for backup. Within what felt like mere seconds, four more cars arrived on the scene. I can't tell you exactly how my roommate and I were separated, but I remember being beaten in an alley. I remember being dragged to my feet and handcuffed. Being tossed into a police car like a bag of old clothes bound for Goodwill. While I gathered myself, I glimpsed several dazed white couples out on Friday-night dinner dates. They weren't paying attention to me, though. I followed their gawking eyes. My roommate was surrounded by club-swinging cops. His arms were raised above his head to block the blows. He wasn't fighting back but he wasn't going down. Finally, a pair of cops tackled his waist and tipped him over. The others piled on. When my friend emerged, he was bloodied and bleary-eyed.

Friday night in a jail cell passed without food or a phone call. The next morning guards woke us up for our arraignment, but when it came time to leave, my friend and I were instead taken to a hospital for treatment of our various bruises and placed in another cell, where we again waited hours without food or water. We never saw a doctor, but we did deduce that we were being held purposefully and likely because someone had figured out that we were law students.

Back at the jail that afternoon, I again asked for and was denied food and water. When I asked for my phone call, I was flat out ignored. The longer I sat in the cell, the foggier everything—the exhilarating freedom I had just experienced in Europe and the bright future I thought lay before me—became. Finally, on Tuesday morning we were herded alongside two dozen other men onto a van. There were no windows, so we couldn't know where we were being driven, though I am certain many of my fellow passengers had taken this ride before. At our final destination, the van parked and the back door swung open. We were ordered to stand up and file out one by one onto a ramp that led directly into a panoptic holding pen in the middle of a wide and open space reminiscent of a vacant warehouse. A hundred or so men who had been arrested over the weekend met the new arrivals with nods, stares, or not all. Men, some hungover or in the early stages of withdrawal, picked fights, pounded their fists on the bars, and mumbled their jumbled thoughts to themselves. Among us captives, a white or Hispanic man lingered here and there, but the vast, vast majority of us were young and Black—me. Among the heavily armed guards the opposite was the case.

Later, after we were herded into a cluster of smaller cells beneath the courtroom, I met with my court-appointed lawyer, also a white man. He read my file and told me that I was being charged with assaulting an officer. The charge carried time—between six months and ten years. My court date would be in the late fall. As the attorney advised me of my options, I started to drift. My nightmare was just beginning.

That night I called my dad. The line went quiet when I broke the news to him. Never a yeller, my old man expressed his greatest disappointments with the cruelty of curtness and silence. For a few days thereafter I walked around thinking I had once again let him down. Then one of his signature, typed letters arrived in the mail. In his way, my dad apologized if he had given me the impression that I was to blame for what had happened to me. "I momentarily lapsed into the belief that we have control over the events that occur in our lives, that we can somehow shape our reality by our behavior," he wrote in a line that still resonates twenty years later, more than fifteen after brain cancer took him from us.

After the letter, my dad secured a defense attorney for me. In our first conversation, I laid out the photos of my bruises and passionately retold the injustices I had endured. My attorney let me go on a while before stopping me. This was serious. The law didn't care if I had been profiled. It wasn't interested in my legal interpretation of my rights. It was my word against the police before a judge who was duty bound to have more faith in the officer's word than that of some Black kid who thought he had rights anyone needed to respect. The best I could hope for, my lawyer told me, was a misdemeanor plea option that would keep me out of jail and come off my record after a period of time. So, as my third year in law school began, I entered the unknown. Was I going to graduate? Would I even be able to take the bar? I went to class every day not knowing what my life would look like the following year. I couldn't make plans, couldn't process the job search. All I could do was not drop out.

My dad flew back from California to join me in court for the trial. As we had a few years earlier when I faced a charge at Rutgers, we drove to the courthouse together. Our lawyer met us on the steps outside the main entrance, and together we passed through security and glided up the escalator to the floor on which our courtroom sat. While my dad and I looked for seats, my lawyer conferred with the prosecutor. Within a few minutes, my lawyer returned holding a document containing a conditional offer: all charges dropped as long as I stayed out of trouble for a year. My record would remain clean. No one would ever know the arrest had taken place. A bitter streak shot through me.

I had waited months to face this lying, petty, vindictive SOB who thought of throwing away my life out of spite. Signing meant I wouldn't get the vindication I longed for. I wouldn't get to tell the cop that what she did was wrong. The system would shield her from accountability for what she had done. My roommate, my lawyer said, wasn't signing. He was fighting on. A wrong had been done to him, to us, and he couldn't stand idly by.

Over the months that followed, I watched the fight take a toll on my roommate. Although we agreed to avoid talking about his trial, I couldn't help but notice when he began exhibiting signs of an emerging mental health condition that would eventually result in his own mother institutionalizing him for a period. He started sleeping all day, missing classes and failing to complete assignments. When he was awake, he'd look out of our living room window for hours without saying a word. I eventually moved out when our living arrangement became untenable. By late spring we'd lost contact. Before I left for New York that fall, a mutual friend shared that he didn't graduate with their class. A decade later I visited my friend in his hometown. He was living in subsidized housing, hadn't held gainful employment in years and refused to use money, calling it "fiat currency." He spent his days reading out of a worn suitcase full of religious texts and drawing elaborate plans for an ashram where he could spread spiritual enlightenment. It's impossible for me to say what happened to him but I know with certainty that he became a different person after the police beating.

At the time, I respected my roommate's choice, admired it, if I'm being honest. But our ordeal had brought me face-to-face with a system that held the indiscriminate power to completely upend my life. I wasn't about to stand trial on principle now that I was being offered the opportunity to put it all behind me. Nor was I about to put my fate in the hands of a system that had, for a second time, so casually tossed my life into turmoil. I knew full well that if I rejected the leniency I was being offered, the system would punish me at trial. So I signed the papers as quickly as I could. Then I swore to my dad that I would do everything in my power to stay out of legal trouble.

On the way out of the courthouse, I counted one Black male after another after another. It occurred to me that we were the coal, the cattle, the cotton—whatever commodity that had once powered this economy—we were part of it now. All the clerks, guards, bailiffs, prosecutors, defense attorneys—even the shoeshine guy—fed their families off our misfortune. Even if the system wasn't designed to feed on Black people, that's what it was doing, and no one seemed the least bit concerned. Whatever doubts I harbored about my decision vanished as we emerged onto the street.

After that, I couldn't unsee the system around me. I had been snatched up by a police officer who knew she had the protection of the law and the backing of the justice system. She used a system that was already well versed in controlling Black bodies to enact racially motivated violence against us. She used the penal code's presumption of her trustworthiness and integrity to violate her oath because she knew she could get away with it. We were just a pair of young Black men. No one would believe us. Yet, take away the badges worn by the dozen officers who clubbed us and we have all of the elements of a hate crime.

Tell me, do you think that as a young white male you would have received the same treatment? Would the cops have even noticed you and your law school buddy fooling around on a street corner? Do the images and ideas about you that live in the public consciousness pose such a threat that the people paid to protect and serve would order you to your knees without a shred of evidence that a crime had taken place? Do you think four more squad cars would have been on the scene as quickly if the dispatcher had said "two Caucasian males" instead of "two Black males"? Would they have wielded their batons as confidently in broad daylight if it were your body's abuse holding the shocked gaze of white onlookers?

What pains me so much about Breonna Taylor's death is that we all know that but for her race, she would still be alive. Rationalizing the judge's decision to grant the cops a no-knock warrant is not helpful. Her ex-boyfriend's suspected underworld ties didn't justify a middle-of-the-night raid on her home. Withholding the grand jury transcripts is purely about protecting a white power structure at the expense of Black pain and suffering.

If Breonna were white, the judge wouldn't have approved a rubber-stamp warrant to a home miles from the cluster under suspicion without some actual proof of her involvement in the conspiracy. If she were white, the cops would have surrounded the house, got on a megaphone, and asked her to come out with her hands up. If she were white, they would not have taken down her door with a battering ram in the middle of the night. We have to accept this as shared truth if we have any expectation of our actions amounting to change.

———

Two summers after my ordeal I found myself sitting in a Texas prison interviewing a young death row inmate, Toronto Patterson. As a juvenile, he had been charged and convicted of killing three relatives, a close cousin and her two small children. He was twenty-four when I met him and slated to die in just a few weeks. I was there as part of a last-ditch effort to convince Governor Rick Perry to spare his life. Toronto and I talked for as long as the authorities allowed.[7] He shared his poetry. He wept for the daughter he'd never see again. He claimed his innocence.

The interview aired on Democracy Now! and generated a modicum of attention but ultimately didn't make any difference for Toronto's life. Two weeks after I met him, I got a call letting me know he was gone. Three years later, the Supreme Court banned juvenile capital punishment. Toronto was the last juvenile put to death in the state of Texas.

Toronto haunted me for the next eight years of my life. Every year on the day of his execution, August 28, the memory of our conversation returned. To the world, he was a murderer who deserved his punishment. Had I not sat across from him and witnessed the fear, loneliness, and despair I had experienced during my brief few days in jail, I might have been indifferent. But I remembered wondering in jail if anyone cared about my whereabouts and well-being. I remembered that while no one around me in jail believed my claims of innocence, I knew the truth, and that made being there worse.

Finally, I gave in and decided to write what ultimately became a book about Toronto's life and death. I found his lawyer, who sent me thousands of pages of court files. I tracked down his criminal record, school records, old poems he wrote to his daughter. I took trips to Dallas to visit his neighborhood and meet people who knew him. On one trip, I retraced the chain of events leading up to the murders and through his arrest later that day. On another, I drove to Huntsville to sit with Toronto's warden, Jim Willett.[8] A perfectly polite man who oversaw eighty-nine executions, Willett in no way thought he had participated in a racist system.

The more I researched, the more holes I found in the story prosecutors told Toronto's jury at trial. Why would he harm the family he clearly loved? The timeline was at best improbable, and an estranged boyfriend had gunpowder residue on his fingers and failed a polygraph. A possible debt owed to the infamous Shower Posse, a gang with a long history of drugs and arms smuggling, might have been the real rationale. Despite the years I spent following Toronto's life and reproducing the crime, I could never decide if he was guilty or innocent. But that just made me wonder even more. How could a jury so casually convict Toronto to die when the evidence of his guilt and the prevalence of systemic racism left so many shadows of doubt?

Right around the time I published *Make Me Believe,* a fictional retelling of Toronto's trial, I found what I have since come to regard as an answer to that question. Out of pure coincidence I met a death penalty lawyer in North Carolina named Ken Rose, who had spent a decade freeing a Black field hand named Bo Jones from death row after proving the star witness for the prosecution had been paid to testify that Jones had killed a white woman.

Rose had been part of a multiracial coalition of death penalty abolitionists who won passage of the North Carolina Racial Justice Act, a now-defunct 2009 law that sought to end racial discrimination in death penalty trials. In a 2011 study commissioned under the law, a pair of Michigan State researchers found that from 1990 to 2010 North Carolina prosecutors in death penalty trials were more than twice as likely to strike qualified Black jury candidates than those who were white. They found that the disparity persisted statewide, by judicial division, and by prosecutorial district. These were important findings because, even at the time, it had long been known that all-white or nearly all-white capital punishment juries convict at higher rates in general, but had a particular predilection for throwing the book at Black people charged with killing white people.[9] In North Carolina, the 2011 study found, all-white or nearly all-white juries were responsible for 40 percent of the death row population.

Defense attorneys such as Ken Rose knew their counterparts had their fingers on the scales. The challenge had always been proving intent. North Carolina prosecutors passed around a "cheat sheet" listing race-neutral explanations for strike decisions, and judges lapped it up every time.[10] The RJA sought to upend that paradigm. Under the law, if a death row inmate could present statistical evidence of racially biased jury selection on the part of prosecutors in the district, judicial division, or state, their penalty was automatically knocked down to life.

So, North Carolina was at least trying to get at a key decision point where systemic racism wreaks havoc. Moreover, the state had used a best-in-class statistical model. But as the saying goes, no good deed goes unpunished. By the time I started flying down to North Carolina to report, the law was already under attack. From the start, the state's forty-four district attorneys had fought passionately against the Racial Justice Act. They took issue with the suggestion that there was racism in their courts and warned the public that millions would be wasted on appeals and experts, not to mention feeding and housing murderers for life.

"Don't get me wrong, I'm not saying that race doesn't influence parts of all systems, because I think it probably does," said Peg Dorer, who directed the state's district attorneys' association. "But to say they were intentionally racially biased is really . . . the DAs find that to be really a repugnant thought and they just object."

GOP leaders also categorically rejected the statistical findings. "I don't believe the DAs across the state—particularly most of whom are Democrats—are racists," state senator Thom Goolsby told reporters just days after the state Senate passed his repeal bill in April 2013.

Dorer's and Goolsby's disbelief helped me make sense of something Bryan Stevenson, who served as an expert witness in the first RJA court hearings, had told me about the law's opponents when we spoke in 2012.

"It's not overt," he said. "I'm not saying anybody hates African Americans. I'm not saying they want to see lynching. They have undeveloped understandings of the ways racial bias manifests itself and plays out in the system of justice. *They've thought very little about it.*"

Sam Sommers, a Tufts psychologist, also spoke as an

expert witness at those court hearings. While reporting on the RJA, I got to know him as well. In his testimony, Sommers told the court that in a jury-selection experiment he conducted, participants were 25 percent more likely to challenge a prospective Black than white juror *even when given the exact same profiles for the two*.[11] That wasn't even his big reveal. Participants in the study overlooked the very attributes and background information—education, job, personal information—in a white prospective juror's profile that they questioned when that same juror profile belonged to a Black prospective juror. Importantly, none—not even one—ever cited race in their explanations. It was always something else.

Stevenson's and Sommers's analyses opened up a door in my brain and shifted the way I have since thought about and approached equity issues. Before I spoke with Stevenson, I was angry. The hypocrisy and willful disbelief of uncomfortable truths astounded and infuriated me. Since speaking with Stevenson, I approach white disbelief as a competency issue. By and large, Americans reflexively reach for a 1960s elixir to treat the modern manifestations of an age-old illness. We focus on *our* intentions. North Carolina prosecutors told themselves that because they were not rejecting Black jurors on explicitly racial terms (i.e., because they were Black), they were free to use an assortment of color-blind rationales that were linked to white-supremacist ideology to strike them from the pool. So, such things as appearance, attitude, dress, body language, and my favorite catchall, "any other sign of a defiance, sympathy with the defendant or antagonism to the State," could legitimately be proffered. But, friend, look closely at those words. They don't have to scream race to mean race. Whose appearance, attitudes, dress, and body language is often negatively stereotyped in the media? *Defiance* is a term often associated with Black folks who speak up or resist white supremacy, is it not? Was it not my "defiance"—asking what law I had broken—that got me beat down? The prosecutors in Toronto Patterson's trial showed the all-white jurors pictures of Toronto wearing gold fronts. They showed the rims on his car. They pulled up his discipline record in school. If not to arouse latent racist ideas that lie like debris across our society, what other purpose did these actions serve?

Black people were once barred from serving on juries in cases involving white people. White supremacy was but one part of the ground upon which that exclusion was legitimately maintained. The corollary was Black inferiority. The two depended on each other. The Civil Rights Act of 1875 secured the rights of Black Americans to sit on juries, but it did not cure the twin maladies, and therefore the law went unenforced. In *Batson v. Kentucky*, more than a century later, the Supreme Court stepped in and explicitly barred prosecutors from excluding Black jurors because of their race. Again, the sickness went unaddressed, therefore prosecutors cooked up cheat sheets to keep Black people off juries.

North Carolina attempted with the RJA to close the loophole with statistical evidence of inequitable capital jury outcomes. Prosecutors and lawmakers pushed back. To say, as prosecutors and the lawmakers who back them knee-jerkedly did, that this is not about racism is not entirely without merit. For someone whose understanding of how racism works is profoundly simplistic, harm to Black communities is never about racism.

Ending structural racism is not only the *erasure* of explicit white supremacy but the *protection* of Black people's rights to participate. It may sound obvious, but we, too, live in this America. It is as much ours as anyone else's. Because you do not approve of how we dress, wear our hair, sit in a chair, or disagree with your views does not give you the right to deny our right to participate in the making of our shared America. Our experiences and the conclusions they may lead us to may be different, but they are not less American. You don't get to beat me up because I stand up for my rights. You don't get to exclude me from service because I may not vote for a death imposition. But most of all, you don't get to live in denial of what you are truly perpetuating because accepting as much puts you at odds with your conscience. *You* have to live with who you are and be okay with that or you have to find the courage to change.

———

A few hours after the Breonna Taylor news landed on us, I met with the employees of one of my clients on a Zoom call. We shared how we felt about the decision. A young white male was the most visibly shaken among us. The summer of protest had opened his eyes. But he said he had friends and family who he knew thought otherwise. "It's the way they were raised," he sighed, shrugging. He didn't mean it. His skin flushed red, his eyes wavered from side to side, and his voice quivered. I didn't envy his predicament. The disbelief necessary to keep loving people who he knew supported racism even if by remaining blind was taxing.

I recognized the young man's reactions. I'd witnessed similar glimpses into a similarly deep inner conflict on the faces of prison guards, wardens, police officers of all ranks, and even an occasional prosecutor. Over the years I covered criminal justice, I met white people who wanted nothing more than to square their beliefs in equality with the unequal social reality that lay before them, yet couldn't. Usually their wall remained intact, but occasionally, often against their intentions, they revealed the psychic toll such a task takes.

"Okay, so if all prosecutors in North Carolina are intentionally racially biased," a flustered Peg Dorer asked me back in 2012, "what are we supposed to do with that? How do you undo that?"

You undo it by first acknowledging that the system is real and you are part of it. That does not mean you created it or actively perpetuate it. It may not even mean you benefit in the ways you have come to believe whiteness is supposed to benefit white people. It just means we all miss things, have gaps in our field of vision, and racism may be yours.

I am not asking for atonement. A public apology would not mean nearly as much to me as you believing Black people when they share the experiences in workplaces, schools, neighborhoods, inside the health care system, with banks. The criminal justice system is merely the most consequential because liberty and life are at stake.

Believe in and trust us not because you feel guilty, but

because we have been telling you our truth for decades, centuries, and those truths might only now be arriving at your doorstep. Rather than assume that ideas and attitudes challenging the systems you have trusted and believed in need to be strangled into submission, consider that this moment of dissonance is valuable data. Maybe the system isn't actually working for you either. Maybe you don't want to keep excusing your racist friends and family. Maybe you also don't agree with the way police treat Black people. Maybe you are ready to stop living in a disbelief.

Audre Lorde once wrote, "We can learn to work and speak when we are afraid in the same way we have learned to work and speak when we are tired."

I do not pretend to think what awaits you will be easy. I know that it will be difficult to exhume the racist ideas you have absorbed, but the culture of disbelief has come at a steep cost to both of us. If you ask me the harm that white disbelief does to you, it is this. It corrupts your relationship with your dignity. It alienates you from your nature. It turns you into your own worst enemy.

III

ACT

Friend,

On April 4, 1968, Martin Luther King's assassination outside of his room at the Lorraine Motel in Memphis triggered a wave of urban unrest. Three weeks later, after rebellions had ripped through dozens of urban centers, Richard Nixon, then still the GOP's presumptive nominee for the president, delivered what was to be his signature appeal to Black America on CBS Radio. In an address entitled "Bridges to Human Dignity, the Concept," Nixon unveiled a plan to grant Black people "a share of the wealth and a piece of the action."[1] Rather than focus on big government that "sought to buy off the Negro" with programs that "perpetuated poverty, and that kept the endless, dismal cycle of dependency spinning from generation to generation," Nixon's Black-capitalism plan centered on local enterprises, small businesses, Black banks, and the like.

What made Black capitalism a remarkable feat of salesmanship was its cynical expropriation of Black Power to win broad support. "We should listen to the militants—carefully, hearing not only the threats but also the programs and the promises," said the man who later told his chief of staff H. R. Haldeman, "The whole problem is really the Blacks."[2]

Unsurprisingly, Nixon's Black capitalism plan turned out to be another hoax. Once in office, he used it to decimate Lyndon Johnson's antipoverty programs while leaving his own newly created Office of Minority Business Enterprise virtually unfunded. Affirmative action, the one initiative that saw tangible gains for the Black middle class, was also the one program that came under the most scrutiny by resentful whites who considered it an infringement upon their rights.

Why am I offering this history? Because we have been at this crossroads before. White Americans—your parents and grandparents—also watched in horror as cities burned. They also awakened to Black anger and pain and promised to do better. And when Nixon offered what they considered an appetizing solution, they devoured it. While the response in Black America was mixed, mainstream white America applauded Nixon's new concept and supported it full stop.

What made Black capitalism so appealing to white people at the time? It cost them nothing, literally and figuratively.

In the 1960s, Black people were demanding an end to segregation. They wanted reparations for slavery. Although whites wanted the unrest to abate and felt genuinely threatened by the Black radical left, they were uninterested in either of those proposals.[3] In that light, Nixon's plan was ideal. It promised to end the government-funded programs that whites resented paying for and believed perpetuated Black dependence. And it charged Black entrepreneurs with solving what were considered Black problems without any committed resources from the very power structure whose policies had left Black communities in disrepair.

Our entire history is littered with examples of the white power structure responding to Black unrest through actions deemed appropriate and acceptable to the white majority. The options presented by Black people themselves are never seriously considered. Perhaps a study will be commissioned or an exploratory committee formed, but in the end, nothing fundamentally changes, certainly not for long, because white people resist.

I hear you loud and clear when you say that you are

ready to take action. I have no doubt that you are deeply unsettled by what you are now unable to avoid seeing, hearing, or feeling. You are restless, anxious, and frustrated. You want action and you want it now. But just as you rightfully question whether a prospective hire has the requisite competence to perform the role for which the person has applied, I earnestly wonder about and am admittedly wary of your readiness claims. I believe that you want me to believe in your desire to take bold action. I even believe that you believe you are ready for bold action. I simply have doubts about your resolve or your sincerity, and you must grant me the legitimacy of those doubts. They are rooted in our historical record. Time and again, generation upon generation, white Americans have responded to the social unrest wrought by racial inequality with great promises of change that have dwindled into window-dressing reforms.

I can't stop you from taking action to right the wrongs you now see. What I can do is caution you from taking action as a knee-jerk response. You feel something happening and you don't know what it is, but you don't want to be left out or behind. You want to be on the right side of history. We all do. We sleep better at night knowing we are not intentionally causing harm. But as you begin or deepen your work, I encourage you to ask yourself a few questions:

Am I doing all of this "work" because I am afraid of losing power and legitimacy? Because I am fearful of being exposed or called out? Or am I doing this because I am truly ready to embrace what's next even if it remains unclear to me? *Be clear about your motivations.*

When it comes to addressing racial (in)equities, what is my deepest desire? Is it the end of systemic racism? Eradicating white supremacy? Is it that we put an end to police brutality? Is it that I find a way to hire more Black people? Support more Black causes? Do I know what Black people want? Are our visions aligned? Do I care? Am I willing to be guided by the desires of those who have faced the most harm? *Be clear about your aims and intentions.*

What does racial justice mean to me? Where does that definition come from? How will I know we have arrived? What does doing better look and feel like? Who gets to decide what doing better is? How is it measured? Where do I see myself in the shortcomings that have led us to this point? What role have I played? *Be clear about your personal history.*

When I think about my spheres of influence—my company, community, and family—what prevented me from taking meaningful action before June 2020? Did I not see the problem? What has changed such that I believe I am ready to show up differently? What am I willing to give—not give up or give away, simply give—so that doing better leads us all to being better? What will keep me from backsliding into complacency? *Be clear about what you are putting on the line.*

I ask these questions from the outset because it is important for me to know if we are truly on the same page in this struggle. And for that to happen, we both need to accept that we have failed in moments of great possibility in our past because we began the journey with different agendas.

If it isn't clear already, Black people aren't fighting just to get better corporate-America jobs. We've heard the empty pledges of inclusion before. Nor will we be satisfied with donations to charity. That money is a drop in the bucket considering all that's been stolen and denied. We are fighting for our mental, emotional, and physical lives. Our nemesis is an arrangement that you thought was perfectly fine up until June 2020 despite the death and despair surrounding you. This arrangement was built on the premise of scarcity and exclusion, winners and losers, victors and vanquished.

We, at least those with whom I align, are building something abundant and inclusive, communal and sustainable, the details of which we are figuring out as we go along.

Thus in this final part I am not going to fall into the trap of telling you what actions you should take. Rather, my intention is twofold. First, I want to introduce and explore *how*, as allies and coconspirators, you can think through and weigh the actions you choose to take. How you choose to act is as important as, if not more than, *what* you choose to do. I present herein a series of problems, situations, and questions that have been presented to me by friends, clients and my own lived experience. Relying on the lessons I've learned as an equity practitioner, I share my thinking—what I consider and how I approach these issues. My intention is to make visible my way of perceiving and to motivate you to think practically about the actions you can take to make change. My assumption is that if you can begin to ask different, deeper questions, then you begin to treat the affliction, not just its symptoms.

The second intention of this final part is to prepare you for the journey ahead. In a speech he gave to teachers the same year Medgar Evers was shot outside his home and four little girls were murdered in a church, James Baldwin wrote, "You must understand that in the attempt to correct so many generations of bad faith and cruelty, when it is operating not only in the classroom but in society, you will meet the most fantastic, the most brutal, and the most determined resistance. There is no point in pretending that this won't happen."

As allies to Black liberation, you will also face resistance. You will face disbelievers. You will encounter friends and family who will reveal to you their truest hearts, and it will be difficult to see them the same thereafter. History has shown that the blowback against Black progress is inevitable. After a period of conciliation, a new generation of white people start to question the wisdom of further investments in Black people. They fret that others—meaning themselves, really—are being victimized by reverse discrimination. Resentment grows and well-meaning whites feel torn between what is right and what is easy.

"Everyone has a plan until they get punched in the mouth," the eminently quotable Mike Tyson once famously said. If you think you have already been punched, think again. There will come a moment when supporting Black Lives Matter will no longer be fashionable. Then, what happens? What do you do when an employee gets arrested at a protest? What about when an employee posts something controversial that causes public scrutiny of your company? How will you address a wealthy client or customer who is utterly opposed to change? What do you do when your children come home radicalized? What happens if someone says the only thing you can do to help as a white person in power is relinquish that power and step aside so others can lead? How will you react then? Where do you draw your line?

As Baldwin writes, there is no point in pretending these things won't happen.

Thus, the final part will raise up some of these questions and encourage you to practice using deep empathy to think through considerations and solutions so that if/when the real moment of truth arrives, you will at least have a frame of reference and clarity on your core values to act in accordance with the beliefs you hold.

———

Corporate America's initial response to the George Floyd uprisings was remarkably swift. Virtual town halls. Speakers. New diversity-hiring commitments. Million-dollar pledges to racial justice charities. Statements supporting Black Lives Matter. It was a moment of action that, once the dust settled, led many organizations to an uncomfortable and uncertain impasse. "Now what?" became the refrain I encountered when white leaders reached out for support. Despite all they had done to show their support and willingness to listen, their people still seemed dissatisfied. Across the board, I encountered dismay and confusion. Were they missing something? Were they not doing enough to show their commitment?

In my experience, men, but especially the white American men with whom I am most familiar, equate action with external activity—something visible and tangible. You look for "quick" or "high-visibility" wins that can be paraded out as evidence that you have the problem under control and are solving it so that all can go back to what they were doing. Typically, those wins can be counted, measured, and crafted into a report through charts produced by experts.

The problem with this approach, and the reason it often led to backlash, was that your own people questioned its inauthenticity. They had always questioned it but had kept quiet for fear of being labeled the angry person of color or simply fired. The summer uprisings merely provided them a megaphone and the protection of public opinion. I discovered as much while hosting focus groups and administering surveys. Time and again, the same set of issues surfaced. The employees of color, too, wanted action, just of a different kind. BIPOC employees especially were unimpressed by the donation to the NAACP when they were still being paid less than their white counterparts. They saw hypocrisy in the company's statement in support of Black Lives Matter when its actual Black employees, the few it had, were nonexistent in leadership roles. They were tired of empty promises of change that typically resulted in one new Black employee or board member. Quite frankly, they were tired of feeling used by powerful white people who had their own agenda.

These employees were urging their employers to look internally and get their own homes in order before making any external promises. Yet when I shared what I was hearing with white leaders, I initially faced blank stares. They didn't see anything wrong with the way things were going. Maybe things needed to be tweaked here and there, but for the most part *they* weren't the problem. The policing system was the problem. Criminal justice was the problem. Whatever it was, the problem was out there, not in here. In contrast, they saw their role as helping to figure out how to leverage their resources to create more opportunity for underserved communities.

Then the data came in and the tune changed. Suddenly, white leaders were ready to listen.

There are a lot of places to begin the internal work, starting with recruitment and hiring practices and cascading through vendor and supplier policies, and many employers are finding success. My approach is a little different. I see diversity, equity, and inclusion as an adaptive challenge. It's not simply something you do as an initiative; it's how you do everything you do. Therefore, writing new job descriptions and revamping the performance-review process is cool, but it will never spread beyond that silo if it doesn't flow from the culture. Culture drives priorities. Priorities determine outcomes. So, for example, employees of color may be recruited and hired, but will they stick around once they get inside? Are you even ready, I ask clients, to hire Black people? How do you know?

Examining culture is the crucial first step because most work environments reflect and value middle-class, white American standards of professionalism without being aware of doing so. Just so we're clear: that's not inherently an issue. But if you are interested in nurturing a more diverse, equitable, and/or inclusive workplace, you're going to want to look at the current status quo. The hardest part of examining white culture is that it's everywhere and in everything, thus it presents as the norm. Without ever having to justify itself beyond nebulous terms such as *fit* or *feeling*, white culture silently dictates appropriate appearance and acceptable behavior. It determines everything from how conflict is handled to how emotion is expressed. Perhaps most important, it decides how business gets conducted.

To be sure, the single most consistent criticism that I read in company survey data and hear in focus groups is that people of color in spaces dominated by white cultural values don't trust their white leaders. They don't per se distrust their leaders because they are white. They distrust because they observe these leaders engage in behaviors that have historically been characteristic of white America's relationship to and treatment of people of color across the globe. In an essay that I frequently use in my work, author and scholar Beverly Daniel Tatum writes, "Dominants do not really know what the experiences of the subordinates is. In contrast, the subordinates are very well informed about the dominants."[4]

Quite bluntly, employees of color have learned to live in a society that has been set up to serve and exalt white males, especially those who present as heterosexual and are of means. We have studied and in some cases learned to mimic this white male ideal as a matter of survival. Because you hold so much wealth and power in this country, we must learn to interact and, far too often, pattern ourselves after you if we hope to get anywhere. That does not mean we believe your approach or your ideas are always right.

You may be thinking, *I am my own person, an individual.* You may take issue with being stereotyped into a single group. I hear and appreciate that sentiment. I certainly don't enjoy being stereotyped into a mass of Black maleness, but I also can't deny that we share common experiences across time and region that link us and that I take pride in. White males also share a common experience. You may identify with your Irish, Jewish, Italian, or Southern roots. To you that's the identity that matters. But to the race-obsessed society we occupy together, it is your white male identity, not your ethnicity, that bequeaths you unspoken, unsolicited advantages that have resulted in a common, convenient blindness to your exalted position. How else do we explain the mass awakening of so many white men of a certain age to the realities of racism in summer 2020? Some are irritated by your ability to live without a named identity. The way you are able to move through the world in a body that solicits respect and elicits rewards pisses off these people. I am not one of them. I don't think of it as a privilege.

As I have watched your unsettling awakening, listened to you search for the language and lenses to name that which for so many people such as me has been apparent for so long, it has occurred to me you are now coming to understand that you have been deprived of a deeper awareness of the price that has been paid to maintain the vast racial inequality that surrounds us. The rationalizations you have been provided to explain your across-the-board advantages over others has made you, at times, brutal and callous, cold and cruel. You have seen your place in the pyramid of existence as a divine right, God's will or the natural order of things. I can't imagine what one must do to keep the dissonance at bay. But now, you are starting to see the horror and want a cure-all. I'm afraid it's not that simple.

So what are the behaviors that employees of color characterize in their experiences of white dominant culture in the workplace? If you are truly interested in a comprehensive list of these behaviors and the ways they manifest, I invite you to read and reflect on Dr. Tema Okun's "White Supremacy Culture."[5] In the surveys I have conducted and the conversations I have had with employees from vastly different organizations, two characteristics in particular stand out. People are fed up with the power hoarding and

the paternalism that defines so many white-led enterprises. Power hoarding shrouds itself in credentials, titles,
reporting relationships, company policies, written rules of
the road essentially, that rationalize those at the top deciding what is best for those down below. It may present
as friendly, meritocratic, even egalitarian, but because its
legitimacy relies on accumulated advantages that whites
disproportionately enjoy as a result of white supremacy, it
is ultimately a means of perpetuating white dominance.

People of color are pushing back hard against this organizational model. They are demanding to be brought into
the process, afforded legitimate space to be heard and contribute and to change the rules to center lived experiences
and impact analyses if need be. They are unwilling to wait
for you to see the value of their contributions. They have
run out of patience for performative adjustments that, to
them, are clearly meant to keep the status quo intact. In
short, they want equity and not just in pay. They believe
they are entitled to accountability and transparency from
the institutions to which they devote their efforts and the
causes that claim they care about racial justice. They believe they ought to be included in decisions that impact
their lives and the lives of those with whom they identify. They want to know if Black people are at the decision-

making table and whether they had a real voice. They want to know what was discussed. They want to hear how those in charge arrived at their conclusions. They want assurances that there wasn't a meeting after the meeting. They want evidence of change, not just promises. They want to see actual, equitable resources allocated to DEI initiatives. They want their feedback acted upon, not just gathered in listening sessions, which paternalistic outfits so often do. They want timely, authentic communication, not to be told after the fact or when it's too late to do anything more than comment. They want honesty from companies that they are giving their time to. They don't want the lone person of color on the leadership team trotted out to talk about the people-of-color issues. They want to hear from the CEO, and then they want to ask questions.

Power hoarding and paternalism are traveling companions, two sides of the same coin. Both have been key features of American expansionism and exceptionalism. Americans have justified our compulsion to conquer and control others with beneficence—we have everyone's best interests at heart, therefore we should be trusted to do what's right. The fallacy of that noble enterprise has been exposed for what it is: neocolonialism or its modern manifestation, neoliberalism. What is left, now, is an opportunity to be and do something different. Emergent models such as stakeholder capitalism are leading the way as are cooperative and shared leadership models. The point is that the times have officially changed. Being the boss no longer means you are entitled to comfortably lord over the masses and reap all of the proceeds without critical feedback. Your people, especially the generations behind ours, do not believe they owe you their loyalty, nor will they show you deference because you hold a title. They will call you out. They will air your dirty laundry. They will embarrass you. So while I cannot tell you what to do, I can tell you the old days of top-down neoliberal leadership are numbered, so it is in your interest to prepare for something new, starting with culture.

So what can you do to adapt? In my practice, I offer clients my LENS framework as a simple starting point.

Listen, learn, and be willing to follow the lead of those with lived experiences in areas you are looking to grow. *Whom do I tend to tune out? Why? What knowledge and wisdom might I be missing out on? How can that knowledge and wisdom benefit us all?*

Draw upon your own experiences of powerlessness and subordination to **empathize** with people who are asking to be seen, heard, and meaningfully included. *What did it* *feel like to be excluded, unseen, undervalued? What did it feel like to be included, seen, valued? What possibilities might be revealed if in moments of tension I use my struggles to seek commonality instead of difference?*

Notice your patterns and reactions to feedback and pushback, especially when it comes from those whose voices and experiences have historically been marginalized. *When do I get defensive? What am I defending in those moments? From whom? Why do I consider "them" a threat? What am I protecting? What am I fearful of losing? Are those fears rooted in scarcity? Is that scarcity an accurate representation of reality? Am I missing an opportunity to choose abundance?*

Speak from the heart. Far too frequently white men in power use silence as a shield or a weapon in race conversations. Time and again I have witnessed powerful white men shut down when they decide an interaction feels too "touchy-feely." When lacking that formal power, I have witnessed white men avoid or retreat from discussions involving race by attempting to intellectualize (analyzing others and not themselves) or by painting themselves as the persecuted scapegoat (often embodied by chronic contrarianism). *Why do I go silent when issues of race come* *up? Why does my fear of saying the wrong thing stop me from engaging? Why do I assume I have nothing to add to the conversation? Why do I prefer analyzing others and resist exploring myself? What can I contribute to the conversation? How can that contribution add to and not derail or detract from the important experiences others are having in this moment?*

Use the LENS framework to build your capacity to see what you have been taught isn't worth seeing. Use it to check yourself in moments of judgment. Use it to feel what others might be feeling. Use it to uncover hidden biases. Use it to shift culture and advance equity. Use it.

Friend,

In the middle of the lone 2020 vice-presidential debate, Mike Pence looked at his opponent, the first Black female candidate for vice president in the nation's history, and questioned the existence of systemic racism.

"This presumption that you hear consistently from Joe Biden and Kamala Harris that America is systemically racist, that, as Joe Biden said, law enforcement has an implicit bias against minorities, that is a great insult to the men and women who serve in law enforcement," Pence said.

As I watched, I could only wonder what it was like for

Kamala Harris to stand there and be lectured on the validity of her life experiences. Repeatedly throughout the night, Pence said that while Harris was entitled to her opinions, she was not entitled to her own facts. Yet, there he stood telling the first Black female attorney general of California, only the second Black female US senator, that racism wasn't real and any suggestion otherwise was offensive.

Let's run the tape. Mike Pence lost his first two bids for Congress. He then took a turn as a conservative talk radio host for a few years. After gaining some notoriety for his evangelical views, he ran for Congress again. This time he won. To his credit, he kept winning. Then he became governor. Then he became vice president. These are all notable but not remarkable feats. Indeed, our nation's history is rife with unremarkable vice presidents. To put a finer point on it, at no point along his career journey was Mike Pence the first to do or be anything. By contrast, at no point in her career—including now as vice president of the United States—has Kamala Harris *not* been a first. Yet, there stood Pence mere days after his boss issued executive order M-20-37 banning all federally funded training on racism as anti-American propaganda, as resolute as ever in his disbelief in the existence of racism.

I can only chalk up that level of certainty in the face of clearly conflicting evidence—Harris was standing just a few feet from him—to willful blindness. Mr. Pence, like so many white men, simply doesn't understand how systemic racism works. And because he doesn't understand it, he is unable to see it even when it is staring him in the face.

My hope is that this letter serves as a tool for those of you who want to see systemic racism in real time.

My wife, Alana, loves the beach. She can lie out in the sun for hours. For the past few summers we have taken at least one extended beach trip. COVID-19 put the kibosh on our annual trip in summer 2020. Nearby Long Island was supposed to be our stand-in, but whenever our work schedules allowed us both to get away from home for a few hours, the weather didn't cooperate.

We finally caught a break in mid-August and drove out to Long Beach on one of those perfect summer Fridays that feel both endless and fleeting. When we arrived, we picked up a bite and headed to the boardwalk. When we got to the beach-access ticket booth, a young woman asked us if we were residents. We'd been to the beach before and already knew that nonresidents had to pay a fee to go on the beach.[6] Alana was reaching for her wallet when the young woman said that we couldn't enter. Baffled, we asked why.

She pointed to a sign. Due to COVID-19, the beach was restricted to residents between Friday and Sunday. We'd driven over an hour and paid a toll only to be told we had to turn around.

My initial reaction was disappointment. The beach was barely occupied, and all we wanted to do was lie out for a few hours. But then the anger descended on me. This new policy called to mind the segregation policies that kept my mother off Buckroe Beach when she was growing up in Virginia. While the sign keeping Alana and me out wasn't intended to enforce the advantages Jim Crow bestowed on white people back then, its effect was no different.

I imagine that sounds alarmist. Clearly the policy was designed to promote social distancing. As such it at least had the legitimate imprimatur of a safety precaution. Moreover, the Monday-through-Thursday access to all meant that no one group was being actively denied beach access; out-of-town beachgoers merely needed to have privileged jobs and/or a lifestyle that would allow them to steal away for a beach day in the middle of the week. *No problem.*

Let's dig deeper.

A cozy enclave with a range of quintessential beach-home styles and sizes, the City of Long Beach sits on the southern tip of Nassau County, one of the most segregated counties in America.[7] Long Beach is the epicenter of that segregation. While the county as a whole is 77 percent white, Long Beach is almost 85 percent white, more than double the white population in nearby New York City.

There's more to the story, though. Long Beach didn't just become one of numerous ultrawhite enclaves on Long Island by mere happenstance. You might have heard of Levittown, the Long Island suburb that famously excluded Black home buyers by legal covenant. Although the Supreme Court invalidated such policies in 1948, William Levitt carried on with his whites-only strategy by wink and nod for another twenty years until, allegedly, Dr. King's assassination provoked him to end the practice as a gesture of respect to the slain leader. By then, it was too little too late. To this day, his suburb remains 90 percent white.

A mere thirty-minute drive south of Levittown, Long Beach's housing history is nearly as checkered. In addition to its own shameful legacy of restrictive covenants, Long Beach initiated a midcentury slum-clearance and urban-renewal program that targeted its Black community.[8] As recently as 2009, a report on housing discrimination on Long Island found that while fair-housing violations were reported across nearly all Long Island's 291 communities between 2000 and 2007, Long Beach was in the top five.[9]

Context is critical to reading systemic racism. Without context, we read a beach policy and assume it's simply a reasonable safety precaution. Adding in the context of the city's history of intentional exclusion complicates the story. The beach policy that turned my wife and me away is suddenly no longer a benign protective measure for residents. It shields accumulated advantages directly linked to racial bigotry. With such a strong racist tailwind, the 2020 policy didn't need to exclude undesirables for its effect to be just that.

Long Beach's beach policy illustrates how intentional racism at a specific time in our past continues to disproportionately advantage whites today *even as it appears to affect all people equally*. No one disputes that explicitly racist policies excluding Black people from living in places of their choosing have officially been scrubbed off the books. Nowadays, even white people may be turned away by a seemingly race-neutral or color-blind policy such as the one we encountered. In our case, even I found myself asking whether the policy was worth making a stink about. We could—and did—just go to another beach. Yet, it is precisely because the policy seems innocent, and an attack on its merits seems unwarranted and unreasonable, that making a stink about it is necessary.

I want to state this emphatically and for the record: Simply because a policy does not *intentionally* seek to harm Black people or negatively affects some white people does not disprove that it is *systemically* racist. If we are only attuned to guarding against the egregious, intentional acts of racism—a white officer targeting a Black body—we overlook the everyday acts the accumulation of which lock us in the same predicament in which our parents and grandparents found themselves. When it comes to understanding and identifying systemic racism, the salient question to ask is whether the existing policy reinforces, sustains, or extends those advantages—material, cultural, or otherwise—that whites initially only accrued as a result of intentional racial bigotry and discrimination. Does the policy protect rights that Black people were unable to access because of racism? Does it preserve privileges that were only available to certain groups of people based on their racial classification? That, I argue, is exactly what was happening at the beach. The racist covenants may have been terminated, but neither the harm that they caused nor the advantages they provided was ever addressed, let alone equitably resolved. Instead, we issue tired apologies and carry on as if that reverses the generations of exclusion. Then we have the nerve to be surprised when we see the racial wealth gap.

In Long Beach, as I imagine is the case elsewhere, because the underlying reparative work—education, examination, economic justice, etc.—was never done, the status quo— the preservation of white entitlement to the local land— remained intact, albeit tacitly. In this light, COVID-19 merely resuscitated a dormant entitlement ethos and rallied it to, once again, keep a beach town that once discriminated on the basis of race "safe" from a new generation of outsiders.

One way to think about the difference between intentional and systemic racism that has been helpful for me is this: the former was about keeping people who were not white behind at all costs; the latter is about keeping white people ahead at all costs. For me, this is the litmus test that matters because, otherwise, systemic racism can appear in such subtle and seemingly innocuous forms that even reasonable people will argue against its validity.

Take car insurance. We all reflexively accept the axiom that premiums are higher in cities than in suburbs. When I moved from a predominantly white suburban community outside New York City back to a predominantly Black community in Brooklyn a few years ago, my rates nearly tripled. When I asked why I was paying so much more when I had only moved forty miles, an agent gave me what sounded like a perfectly reasonable explanation. The risk was higher in Brooklyn. Yes, I said, but three times higher?

A year later ProPublica published an investigation into car insurance premiums and payouts across four states, California, Illinois, Texas, and Missouri.[10] It chose those states because, well, those were the only four that made publicly available the data necessary for geographic comparison. ProPublica's investigation revealed startling disparities in premium prices offered to similarly situated white and Black Americans that could not be explained by the differential costs that insurance companies incurred in white and Black communities. Put differently, insurance companies have long insisted that their premiums are set based on the risk of loss, but ProPublica's findings contradicted that assertion. It instead found that wherever the geographic data was available, insurers were charging motorists in Black neighborhoods higher premiums than motorists in similar white neighborhoods. In one particularly blood-boiling instance, ProPublica found that a young Black father who was barely getting by was paying GEICO four times as much to insure his ten-year-old Honda than a white male advertising executive was paying to insure his late-model luxury SUV even though GEICO paid out less in accident claims in the father's Chicago neighborhood.

Here's what we know and is not in dispute: Insurance companies, like beaches, once intentionally denied access to Black people. Then laws were passed banning discrimination. Yet, here we are anyway looking at evidence corroborating what so many people such as me have long suspected—that race is still intertwined with insurance-premium pricing—that if you are Black or live around Black people, you pay more regardless of whether the community you live in poses a higher risk to insurers.[11]

Unsurprisingly, when presented with the findings, insurance insiders either ignored ProPublica's request for comment, challenged the methodology of the data, or vehemently denied discriminating on the basis of race. And why wouldn't they? The current arrangement works for shareholders. Legendary investment wizard Warren Buffett has called GEICO his "favorite investment" of all time.[12] At least some portion of the billions Buffett has made from GEICO came by way of discriminatory premiums in communities of color, yet when pressed about placing people of color on search committees for board and CEO seats, he balked.[13] Does that inconsistency make Buffett a racist? I don't know. I prefer to simply say that like so many of his peers who resist firm commitments to diversity because the whiff of a quota makes them queasy, he is unable to see how he has benefited from racism built into the structure of our society.

In America, race and geography are interwoven. The enduring patterns of segregation we see in our country are a direct result of widespread, well-documented housing discrimination efforts that have been further exacerbated by employment discrimination and education inequity. It is all linked in a seamless chain across our collective life cycle. Thus, the insurance industry need not "discriminate on the basis of race"[14] for its risk-assessment algorithms to compute extortionate rates in Black communities. The problem is that those algorithms don't account for disinvestment, militaristic policing, education-funding inequity, chronic underemployment, and the like that are rooted in racism. Those algorithms weren't built to give due weight to the past. Likewise, the industry need not grant bonus points based on credit scores, education, and occupation with the intention of advantaging whites and punishing people of color who have historically been denied access for that to be the outcome. When you insert context into the equation, you begin to see how unfair these practices are and how they can perpetuate the very things we want to eradicate.

I know, it's overwhelming. It feels like an unsolvable problem. Can't we just focus on doing better moving forward? Let bygones be bygones. Forgive and forget. No, I'm afraid we can not. Although our forward-looking orientation has served us well as a country, we must interrogate and integrate the injustices of our past into our current understanding of the problems we are trying to solve if we are ever going to reconcile. Moreover, we should not be asking people who have again and again been given a bad check to just let go and get over. Not when the crimes of the past are in the present continuing to reap rewards for some and create hardships for others.

Here is the thing: If we don't tackle all of it, get into the innards of the tangled web we've woven around racial caste and disentangle every form in which it appears, if we don't take the time for careful consideration of our actions and whom they harm and benefit, then we are doomed. If we don't eradicate explanations and justifications—beliefs often unfounded by the data—rooted in racism but cloaked in code words and dog whistles, then Black people will always be carrying a disproportionate burden even as white people insist they are the ones being asked to shoulder the load. We don't get to choose which policies we want to fix and which we can leave be. We don't get to rank their importance because the alternative is too tedious. We simply need to learn to use new approaches and new tools to conduct our affairs.

It is no secret yet it is rarely said in public that white males are still very much in charge of America. Across every sector of society, white males are disproportionately represented in senior leadership and decision-making roles.[15] I do not expect nor am I asking these men to simply hand over power. I operate with the assumption that the vast majority are qualified for the positions they hold. Where I struggle and have legitimate concerns is with their ability to fully appreciate how the systematic exclusion and exploitation *of* Black people has been rationalized into a problem *with* Black people.

In a conversation with employees following the murder of George Floyd, Wells Fargo CEO Charles Scharf explained that the bank's paucity of Black senior leaders was due to a "very limited pool of Black talent to recruit from."[16] Scharf made his remarks with earnest intention but without facts to corroborate them. Instead of making sure he had accurately diagnosed the issue before speaking, he relied on his limited experience and understanding, assuming neither were colored by racist ideology. Troublingly, Scharf has held top posts at JPMorgan, Citigroup, BNY Mellon, and Visa. He sits on the board of Microsoft and Johns Hopkins. All of which is to say, he has moved from one elite institution to another, and only now is he being challenged to consider if his beliefs about the absence of Black talent may have been inaccurate.

By and large, the white males in charge of society's powerful institutions have not needed to know about race and racism to get to the top. Their boards and shareholders have not held them accountable to diversity goals, and they have not been asked to take deeper looks into the inequities that their enterprises exploit or exacerbate. Suddenly, they need not only empathy and a willing ear but actual competence. Without it, their people won't trust. And without that trust, they can't lead.

These are the stakes. At home and in your communities, they are just as high.

So how do you reconcile this gap should you find yourself standing on the precipice of uncertainty looking down at the abyss and wondering how you get to the other side intact? Here are my parting suggestions:

———

Get a grip. The movement for racial justice isn't about you or whether you think you are being unfairly targeted for recompense. The price of unchallenged dominion such as white males have experienced in America is the thin skin you walk around with. You are not used to being challenged, and, yes, it stings, but it does not compare to the existential anxiety Black parents face each time their child walks out the door into the arms of a world that has many times over proven its antipathy to their existence. As a corollary, avoid seeking equivalencies. Reverse discrimination can happen, and when it does, it is wrong. But as researchers studying the effect of affirmative action policies have found, whatever harm individual white people may experience in, for instance, not getting into their top-choice school is largely illusory, since less than 20 percent of colleges and universities overall and only 6 percent of the most selective schools even consider race in admissions.[17] Most white males aren't even applying to the top schools in America. The point: If you are a white male, it is highly unlikely that you have been discriminated against or will ever be, especially to the degree Black people have been.

———

Buckle up. Either we're going to be in this work of reconciling and healing for a while or our children will be. If our own upbringing can tell us anything, it's this: chanting we're not racist doesn't work. Racial justice is going to take a long time, and it is going to be messy at times. Feelings will be hurt. Mistakes will be made. Diversity efforts will fail. None of that is a reason to turn away. We don't quit on relationships when they hit a snag or disappoint us. We dig in. We get creative. We have to see this endeavor as essential, not mandatory. As a prerequisite to our collective destiny, not a requirement to clear our conscience. As long as the Black-white wealth divide remains as wide as it was the day Martin Luther King died, we have work to do. As long as race determines everything from education to health outcomes to longevity, we have work to do. As a corollary, find your beauty in the struggle. If you only see racial justice as an arduous task of unlearning and learning, then it will feel like work. When you are able to experience the benefits of social-justice labor—authentic, trust-based relationships across difference; an awareness of the absurdity of a caste system designed to advantage and disadvantage based on skin color—you will feel a sense of levity that isn't dependent on blindness.

———

Look back on your life. Since we are going to be in this racial-justice reckoning for a while, you may as well get comfortable. Start by looking back at your life. I offered my experience growing up Black inside white institutions so that perhaps you could tap into your own experiences in those spaces as well. Now it's your turn. When thinking about the beliefs you hold about race, where and when were they formed? What happened? Who else was involved? A parent? A grandparent? A teacher? A pastor? What role did you play? Were you a perpetrator, bystander, a victim? Were you silent? Did you turn away? Did you act? What did those moments teach you about race and racism? About who you are and who I am? About who is worthy and who is unworthy? How do those past moments continue to influence you today? Have they created barriers to empathy, left gaps in your understanding, made it difficult for you to act? Have they made you angry at Black people? Annoyed at us? Exhausted by our demands? Do you take pity on us because you grew up believing we needed saving? Do you ignore our pain because somewhere along the way you were taught that we deserve the mistreatment we have experienced? These are hard questions, I know, but if you want to do better, you must start by interrogating your past to see what's there and whether it is still serving you.

———

Resist the urge to turn away. Have you ever left a theater in the middle of a movie or performance? We all have. But has anyone left in the middle of *your* performance? I once started a race and racism workshop for a nonprofit board with twenty-five people and finished an hour later with fewer than fifteen. Not one of them said goodbye. Not even in the Zoom chat. This wasn't even my most racy race workshop. All I did was talk about redlining—that's it. And still, ten white people who sat on a board whose mission was serving youth of color from a low-income community couldn't be bothered. They each just clicked the "leave meeting" button and disappeared. Poof. Back to the comfort of their lives. It was that easy to tune out the Black man because it's always been that easy to tune out Black people. Whenever white people haven't liked the message, they've had the privilege to turn away. But turning away comes at a cost.

If you are truly committed to this struggle, then you are going to need to get comfortable with discomfort. This isn't to say you should endure verbal abuse because you are a white male or sit through conspiratorial racist rhetoric that has no basis in fact. It does mean that discomfort is not the same as discrimination. Mike Pence's indignation at the mere suggestion of systemic racism does not compare to the legitimate barriers Kamala Harris had to navigate to reach that same stage.

Friend, you are going to have to learn how to hear truths that might challenge your view of the world or present you with information that you didn't know, such as that the electoral college is a vestige of slavery.[18] These truths may be spoken by people you have been conditioned to doubt and dismiss because of their skin color or gender expression or lack of letters behind their name. You are inevitably going to think to yourself that there is just no way this Black person knows more about American history than you do. You're going to want the article or book he or she is referring to so you can read it for yourself. You're going to want to resist. And in that moment, you will have a decision to make. Use the discomfort as data to interrogate your resistance or click the "leave" button. Leaving is your right. Just know that when you do so just because you don't like the message, you are part of the problem.

Corollary: Joining a charity board does not grant you immunity. Look under the hood. The Black staff may be miserable.

———

Resist distraction. Black-on-Black violence and police violence are not two sides of the same coin. Do not fall into the false-equivalency trap. It's tempting because it appeals to the deeply held but rarely spoken belief that Black people use racism as an excuse for their moral failures. Because Black people speak out against one and don't speak about the other as much as you think we should does not mean Black people don't care about what is going on in the community. It might just mean that one is a community issue and the other is a municipal issue. The police are a publicly funded institution. Police are trained at the expense of the *public*. Police are paid with *public* dollars. They are granted unique privileges. We have the collective authority to change policing, so let's focus on that. Don't get consumed with what's happening in the Black community and what the right solution should be. Assume you don't know or understand what's going on. Accept that no one is asking you to diagnose what's wrong with a community that you have never been a part of or taken an interest in. Focus on what is being asked of you.

Corollary: If the looting of stores angered you more than the shooting of Black bodies, then you need to sit with yourself for a moment and ask why you value replaceable property more than Black life.

Corollary II: Because a Black social activist earns money through her activism does not mean she is pimping poverty or is a race hustler. It may mean she has a family to feed, student loans to repay, and a future to plan for. Activism alone does not pay the bills. Besides, you expect to be paid for your labor, so why shouldn't a Black activist be paid for hers? Don't discredit the message or the messengers because they know their value and aren't giving themselves away for free to satisfy your purity standard. Again, you may need to sit with yourself for a moment and ask why this bothers you in the first place.

———

Focus on race. If I've heard it once, I've heard it a thousand times. Your company wants to tackle diversity, but it doesn't want to focus only on race. It wants to be wider. Wants to cover *all* forms of diversity. If that sounds like you, my question is, What are you afraid of? Why does a focus on race repel you? Whom and what are you protecting? The Thirteenth, Fourteenth, and Fifteenth Amendments were passed because Black people struggled for their freedom. Now everyone benefits. The Civil Rights Acts of 1964 and 1965 were passed because Black people struggled for their rights. Now everyone—even white people—benefit.[19] History has shown that focusing on Black people yields benefits to all. I'm insulted when people tell me that focusing on race is too narrow. Race is the mother ship. In this country, nothing else is more divisive or defining. The color line remains the cornerstone of capitalism. History has shown us time and again that if you solve for race, then you solve for everything else.

Corollary: It's not a pipeline problem. It's a race problem. Black talent is out here. You just have to be willing to invest in it.

———

Focus on impact. At the height of the pandemic one of my clients laid off nearly 50 percent of its employees. I asked the COO how the organization had decided who would be let go. He said they looked at who was and wasn't essential. Because programs were on pause, the people who ran them were no longer essential. For context, 90 percent of the program staff was of color. By contrast, 75 percent of the administrative and leadership staff was white.[20] The result of the decision was that twenty-seven of the twenty-eight layoff casualties were people of color. The COO said that while he felt bad about the decision, he didn't see any other choice. Those people just weren't necessary.

An organization or leader committed to equity has to be willing to see and make other choices. Business as usual has resulted in people of color remaining underrepresented in leadership and overrepresented in lower-paid, more conveniently expendable roles. It has resulted in Black people experiencing higher rates of unemployment and disproportionately bearing the burden of mass layoffs.

The organization could have prevented the decision from having a disproportionate impact on one group by conducting an impact analysis *before* the layoffs occurred. It could have looked at the data. It could have reminded itself that structural racism results in Black people having less access to education and opportunity, lower-paid, more vulnerable jobs, and higher rates of unemployment. It could have seen and seized the moment to stand in its anti-racist values.

Could certain high performers be trained up? Were any role-sharing options available? Were certain high-paying, senior-level roles automatically protected from scrutiny or deemed untouchable when they didn't need to be? If so, is that fair to the process?

This may feel uncomfortable. It may strike too close to

home or run counter to your sense of how business should be conducted. The thing is, the current arrangement is broken. Tweaks won't fix the mess we are in. An inequitable system cannot be made more equitable without some discomfort. Not when every economic indicator tells us inequality is getting worse. We need new, bold measures. We need to take real risks, and as long as you focus on your good intentions, we won't. We will keep getting the same results. Instead, in key moments focus on the historically harmed and what actions you can take to prevent their being harmed again.

———

Share the power. When a nonprofit CEO faced an internal staff revolt over the organization's reliance on quantitative success measures, I advised him to form a working group of junior staff of color and allow them space to develop some new success measures. Give them the support they need, I said. And when they are ready, pilot their ideas. If they work, great. If they don't, at least you'll know. The next day the CEO told me that he was initially taken aback by my recommendation. He wasn't about to let the staff decide the measures of success. That was *his* job. He was the

CEO. He decided the big, important things. Then he slept on it. When he woke up, he had a change of heart. The worst that could happen is the measures wouldn't succeed. On the other hand, they might unlock something that could accelerate the company.

———

Don't expect Black people to be the savior. White men have been in charge of America since its inception. Being in charge means you call the shots. It means you decide whose ideas are and are not worth investing in and giving room to fail. White American men have been incredibly, awe-inspiringly successful. White men have also been granted the collective and institutional trust and resources to fail and fail again. Black people, as well as many other identities, have never been granted that space to fail. And when you are not given space to fail, you are also not given space to succeed.

We have to be honest and admit that Black leadership is typically sought out and brought in only when all else fails and the company (or country) needs someone to turn things around. We get the big job in part because everyone figures it's a fool's errand. We get it because only a miracle worker can right the ship. We get it because there's literally nothing left to lose. Think about Barack Obama's presidency. He inherited an economy in tatters. He had two drawn-out wars to wind down. For many Black people, his experience mirrored their own. We walk into a house on fire because we have to. Because if we don't take the once-in-a-lifetime opportunity even if it isn't ideal, we won't get another chance down the line.

This feeling became particularly relevant for me when companies far and wide started reaching out for DEI services. They all wanted someone yesterday. They were having problems and they needed someone to solve them right away. I was that someone. Do not hold me to a perfection standard. Not everything I try will be a hit. Not every idea I offer will be brilliant. Just because you are not seeing change as quickly as you anticipated or think is necessary doesn't mean it isn't happening or won't happen or that I have failed. Practice patience with me. Allow for the same experimentation and iteration that we allow for when it comes to developing products. I didn't create racism, so don't expect me to solve it in your organization in six months.

———

Consider stepping down. For a few weeks in June 2020 it felt as if no white male CEO was safe. Every day offered up a new headline. Some white CEOs clearly needed to step down. They were toxic and causing harm to their companies. Others, though, didn't see themselves as possibly being part of the problem. If that sounds like you, then it is to you whom I address this message: If you are genuinely uncertain how to lead your people through this moment, you should consider if you are the right person for the job. I mean this. A CEO of an international firm whose sales are driven by its products' popularity in the Black community wanted to hire me to be his personal DEI adviser. He envisioned me sitting in on meetings with him. Fielding questions for him. Essentially, he wanted me to teach him how to do his job when, in reality, the job itself had changed, and he was no longer qualified. I said no thank you.

DEI competency is not something a CEO or board member should be picking up on the job. How so many white men have made it through life without ever interacting with American history or understanding how their racial identity has given them advantages is beyond me. The time for that has come and gone. If you can't communicate with your staff on issues that are core to their existence, then you are just not qualified. If you don't understand the consumers who drive your brand, then you are also not qualified. DEI competency is an essential skill that those around you shouldn't have to wait for you to gain now that your eyes are open.

There is a certain irony to all of this. So many Black people don't get senior-level opportunities in the first place because they "lack the requisite experience"; yet now that so many white leaders lack the experience to lead on DEI, we are willing to give them all the additional training and coaching they need to get up to speed. What if the proper, just, and responsible thing to do is just step down and make space for leaders who have those skills?

————

This is about the next generation. A 2019 EdBuild report showed that in America, predominantly white schools receive on average $2,000 more per child per year than their majority-minority counterparts. Multiply that $2,000 by five hundred students and we're talking $1 million. This is real money with real implications. It affects teacher pay, which affects teacher quality, which affects student achievement. It affects classroom size, which affects student discipline and student achievement. A recent study out of Stanford identified a correlation between the racial discipline gap and the racial achievement gap. In school districts where the discipline gap between Black and white students was higher, so, too, was the academic achievement gap. The reverse was also true.[21] Why is this relevant? This is exactly what our parents' generation did, the mistake they made. Why we continue to remain estranged from one another.

Choosing to limit your tax dollars to your local community harms communities of color. There is no uncertainty about that. When it comes to education access, local tax policies are the great unequalizer. Moving out of one neighborhood to place your child in a better school in another neighborhood deprives one community of tangible resources and over-advantages another. Resisting attempts to integrate public schools because you want your child to attend the best school money can buy is opportunity hoarding.[22]

I know you will say it is more complicated. That I would make the same decision if it were my child I was talking about. My response is that I understand, but this is the crossroads where our democratic values and liberty interests meet; where our ideas of who we are bump up against our lived values. My only intention throughout this little book has been to hold up a mirror. If we want a different future, then we have to be willing to make decisions with risks. You are going to have to put something on the line. I don't expect most of you reading this to be willing to do that, and while that is okay, it must also be named for what it is. You don't get to know the racism is real, do nothing about it, and still claim you are on the side of justice.

In my writing of this book, a group of white men—some I knew, a few I didn't but who reached out after reading my work—organized themselves into a white men's study group. The organizer, a colleague and friend on the younger side of the "certain age" range to whom I initially directed the letter that spawned this book, had put together a ten-week syllabus that he asked me to review and give feedback on. I was impressed by its rigor and candor. He wasn't pulling punches. I admittedly wondered how many white men would accept his challenge. When a few weeks later he told me about the enthusiastic response, I was amused, amazed, and a little alarmed. As cool as the idea was of a group of white men gathering to talk about whiteness, white-supremacy culture, and how they could become allies and accomplices to racial justice, I wondered what it would amount to and whether this was the appropriate response to the call I'd issued in my initial letter. Was white men talking to one another about their experiences the right move? By and by, I realized that it wasn't up to me. I'd put out a call, and a group of white men had answered. The rest was on them. This was their work.

Halfway through the group's schedule, I was invited to join one of the weekly Zoom calls to talk about race in the workplace. I decided to talk about what it would mean and look like to focus on impact instead of intention. We looked at Supreme Court cases, laws, definitions, and data. At the end of the call, which had capped a long day of calls, I walked downstairs to join Alana for dinner.

"How did it go?" she asked excitedly.

"We made the best of it, I suppose," I said somewhat perfunctorily.

"Is that *all*?"

The edge in her voice jarred me. Actually, this was a big deal and not just because they were this book's exact audience. In the thick of what quite likely will be viewed as our generation's signature moment of racial reckoning, we held space to hear one another's experiences and perspectives across a chasm that has caused so much pain and confusion for so many generations of Americans. They were a small group—ten total—and mostly on the liberal side of the spectrum, but their size and politics were irrelevant. A Black man had written what might be considered a harsh letter to his white friends, and rather than turn away from its truth, rather than reject, deny, or defend, they were choosing vulnerability and reflection. Rather than throw themselves headlong into action—a classic work-avoidance technique—they were acknowledging their knowledge gaps and taking time to learn together. Rather than insist they could walk this difficult journey on their own or leaning on their Black friends to teach them, they had agreed to hold one another accountable and carry their weight in our collective destiny.

"I don't want to get ahead of myself," I said to Alana, "but I think these guys may be stepping up."

ACKNOWLEDGMENTS

My mother and mother-in-law, Evelyn and Yvonne. Thank you for always lifting up my light when others did not and just loving on Ella, Alana, and me.

My big sisters Leslie Amina and Candace, nieces Laila and Mia, nephews Joseph and Josh, and brothers Jay, Doug, and Phillip. Thank you for being such incredibly talented, resilient, accomplished, and decent people that I am always able to draw inspiration from.

Byrd Leavell. Thank you for always taking my calls, answering my emails, showing up as a friend first and earnest, critical literary agent second. And thank you for believing I had a second act in me.

Rico Blancaflor and Chirag Menon—my Third Settlements brethren. Thank you for holding it down while I disappeared to write. Thank you for being great artists, designers, partners, and humans.

Mike Wood, Jamie Krents, Pete Sisitsky, Eric Single-tary, Mark Raspberry, and Natalie Randolph—my Sidwell crew. Thank you for taking the time to reminisce on our childhood and explore our shared histories.

Jason Spector, Aaron Dworkin, and Emely Marti-nez—my All-Stars crew. Thank you for cocreating new frontiers for collaboration.

Cassi Feldman, Taya Kitman, Sarah Blustain, Mark Rochester, and Esther Kaplan—my Type Media Center family. Thank you for providing me with a home, scrupu-lous editing, and the space to pursue my passion.

Daniela Rapp and the entire St. Martin's Press team. Thank you for offering me such an amazing platform to publish this book and, then, giving me the space to say what I needed to say.

George Suttles and Cyndi Suarez. Thank you for the hours we spent building, breaking bread, and for sharing my work with your incredible networks. #NonprofitWakanda

Finally, all of the people—friends and strangers alike—who read the original letter, passed it along to others, and reached out to let me know what it meant for them. Were it not for those encouraging reactions to a letter I had only intended to share with a few friends, this book would not exist. Thank you.

NOTES

I. HARM

1. http://www.city-data.com/zips/20016.html.
2. https://www.pewresearch.org/fact-tank/2020/04/28 /millennials-overtake-baby-boomers-as-americas-largest -generation/.
3. https://www.prb.org/usrecessionandbirthrate/.
4. https://www.dcpolicycenter.org/publications/regional -population-density-since-1970/.
5. https://www.nytimes.com/1972/05/17/archives/wallace-off -the-critical-list-sweeps-primary-in-michigan-and-wins.html.
6. https://www.npr.org/sections/ed/2016/10/05/495504360 /looking-back-on-50-years-of-busing-in-boston.
7. https://www.thedailybeast.com/how-a-1973-supreme-court -decision-has-contributed-to-our-inequality.
8. https://www.washingtonpost.com/posteverything/wp/2014/07 /24/youve-probably-never-heard-of-one-of-the-worst-supreme -court-decisions/.
9. https://www.census.gov/library/stories/2020/09/poverty-rates -for-blacks-and-hispanics-reached-historic-lows-in-2019.html.

10. https://www.nytimes.com/1983/06/19/us/study-says-affirmative-rule-expands-hiring-of-minorities.html.

11. https://digitalcommons.law.scu.edu/lawreview/vol35/iss2/5/.

12. https://www.latimes.com/archives/la-xpm-1987-05-01-me-1592-story.html.

13. https://www.washingtonpost.com/archive/politics/1994/06/10/retired-justice-changes-stand-on-death-penalty/9ccde42b-9de5-46bc-a32a-613ae29d55f3/.

14. In this specific instance, Scalia meant that he saw no evidence that the Transportation Authority had discriminated in the past, therefore its affirmative action plan couldn't have been conceived to address actual discrimination. This presumes that we have a shared understanding of and agreement on what those actual harms are. I'm not confident Justice Scalia or most white men share my understanding of harm or of how they have been advantaged by it.

15. This is essentially the argument that the current chief justice, Roberts, made when in 2007 he wrote, "The way to stop discrimination on the basis of race is to stop discriminating on the basis of race."

16. For more on its fall, see https://www.wilsonquarterly.com/stories/the-rise-and-fall-of-the-american-melting-pot/.

17. Read more here: https://theshadowleague.com/still-fighting-the-stereotypes-that-doug-williams-smashed-30-years-ago/.

18. https://shelterforce.org/2004/05/01/reagans-legacy-homelessness-in-america/.

19. Washington, a Black D.C. Police Academy applicant, claimed that the department's test was biased because it asked culturally specific questions that Black people were less likely to know the answers to. His main evidence was the disproportionate failure rate of Black applicants. The Supreme Court ruled that his equal protection rights had

not been violated because he could not prove that the department had intentionally sought to discriminate on the basis of race.

20. https://www.washingtonpost.com/archive/opinions/1989/01/22
    /hold-on-john-thompson-the-prop-42-flap-ducks-the-real-problems
    -in-black-education/b099a62d-2c38-4622-92b4-3b6a99bdfb49/.

21. https://www.aera.net/Newsroom/Teachers-Are-People-Too
    -Examining-the-Racial-Bias-of-Teachers-Compared-to-Other
    -American-Adults.

22. https://archive.news.indiana.edu/releases/iu/2016/05/gifted
    -student-placement.shtml   and   https://blogs.edweek.org/edweek
    /rulesforengagement/2017/10/teachers_lower_expectations
    _for_black_students_may_become_self-fulfilling_prophecies
    _researchers_say.html.

23. https://www.usatoday.com/story/news/education/2019/02/04
    /black-history-month-february-schools-ap-racism-civil-rights
    /2748790002/.

24. https://www.apa.org/research/action/stereotype.

25. https://www.huffpost.com/entry/imposter-syndrome-racism
    -discrimination_l_5d9f2c00e4b06ddfc514ec5c.

26. https://www.sciencedaily.com/releases/2007/09/070919093316
    .htm.

27. https://www.nytimes.com/1991/08/01/us/naacp-and-top-labor
    -unite-to-oppose-thomas.html.

28. https://www.newyorker.com/culture/essay/clarence-thomass
    -radical-vision-of-race.

29. https://amp.theatlantic.com/amp/article/378162/.

30. https://www.epi.org/publication/the-growing-use-of-mandatory
    -arbitration-access-to-the-courts-is-now-barred-for-more-than-60
    -million-american-workers/.

31. https://ropercenter.cornell.edu/how-groups-voted-1988.

32. https://ropercenter.cornell.edu/how-groups-voted-1992.

33. https://www.ncbi.nlm.nih.gov/pmc/articles/PMC1376990/; https://www.intelltheory.com/bellcurve.shtml.

34. https://www.nytimes.com/1994/10/09/magazine/daring -research-or-social-science-pornography-charles-murray .html?searchResultPosition=1.

35. https://www.nytimes.com/1995/02/06/nyregion/a-career-in-the -balance-rutgers-s-president-starts-a-firestorm-with-three-words .html.

36. https://papers.ssrn.com/sol3/papers.cfm?abstract_id=1692879.

II. HEAL

1. https://www.ams.usda.gov/sites/default/files/media /Poultry%20-%20Guidelines.pdf.

2. https://archive.org/stream/countryschooloft00gates?ref =ol#page/n5/mode/2up/search/in+our+dreams.

3. https://cityroom.blogs.nytimes.com/2011/10/27/income -disparity-is-greatest-in-new-york-census-finds/.

4. https://www.nytimes.com/2011/06/12/realestate/hamilton -heights-awaiting-a-bounce.html?pagewanted=all.

5. https://www.csmonitor.com/1996/0319/19202.html.

6. https://www.brookings.edu/research/envisioning-a-future -washington/.

7. https://www.youtube.com/watch?v=9aLnP6g1OK4&ab _channel=Dax-DevlonRoss.

8. https://vimeo.com/19097232.

9. See https://www.nytimes.com/1987/04/26/weekinreview/racial -challenge-rejected-court-stands-behind-the-death-penalty.html

and https://www.nytimes.com/1998/06/07/us/new-study-adds-to-evidence-of-bias-in-death-sentences.html.

10. http://www.ncids.org/Motions%20Bank/RacialJustice/BatsonJustification.pdf. The explanations include appearance, attitude, dress, and body language and "any other sign of a defiance, sympathy with the defendant or antagonism to the State."

11. https://www.hbs.edu/ris/download.aspx?name=sommers%20norton%20race-based%20judgments.pdf.

III. ACT

1. https://www.presidency.ucsb.edu/documents/remarks-the-cbs-radio-network-bridges-human-dignity-the-concept.

2. https://archive.org/details/isbn_9780199793747.

3. In his 1969 annual report, FBI director J. Edgar Hoover wrote, "The Black Panther party, without question, represents the greatest threat to the internal security of the country." https://cdnc.ucr.edu/?a=d&d=DS19690716.2.89.

4. https://uucsj.org/wp-content/uploads/2016/05/The-Complexity-of-Identity.pdf.

5. https://collectiveliberation.org/wp-content/uploads/2013/01/White_Supremacy_Culture_Okun.pdf.

6. The privatization of public resources is another conversation for another time.

7. https://projects.newsday.com/long-island/segregation-real-estate-history/.

8. http://eraseracismny.org/storage/documents/housing/Long_Island_Fair_Housing_a_State_of_Inequity.pdf.

9. http://eraseracismny.org/storage/documents/housing/ERASE_Housing_reportcard_final_2009.pdf.

10. https://www.propublica.org/article/minority-neighborhoods-higher-car-insurance-premiums-white-areas-same-risk.

11. In summer 2020, the National Association of Insurance Commissioners agreed to review car insurance rates for racial bias. https://content.naic.org/article/news_release_naic_announces_special_committee_race_and_insurance.htm.

12. https://www.fool.com/investing/2019/12/29/heres-how-much-money-warren-buffett-has-made-in-ge.aspx.

13. https://finance.yahoo.com/news/buffett-rejects-diversity-measure-but-throws-support-behind-its-goal-001730183.html.

14. This was the explanation to ProPublica by the Insurance Information Institute, an industry trade association.

15. https://www.nytimes.com/interactive/2020/09/09/us/powerful-people-race-us.html.

16. https://www.nbcnews.com/news/nbcblk/wells-fargo-ceo-ruffles-feathers-comments-about-diverse-talent-n1240739.

17. https://www.washingtonpost.com/nation/2018/10/19/most-white-americans-will-never-experience-affirmative-action-so-why-do-they-hate-it-so-much/.

18. https://www.theatlantic.com/ideas/archive/2019/11/electoral-college-racist-origins/601918/.

19. https://www.nytimes.com/2009/06/30/us/30scotus.html.

20. https://www.eeoc.gov/employers/small-business/avoiding-discrimination-layoffs-or-reductions-force-rif.

21. https://phys.org/news/2019-10-relationship-racial-discipline-disparities-academic.html.

22. https://www.washingtonpost.com/opinions/local-opinions/montgomery-countys-public-schools-are-still-segregated-its-time-to-fix-that/2020/07/02/8541a08c-b65a-11ea-aca5-ebb63d27e1ff_story.html.